THE

BAROMETER OF THE SOUL

SO

Be Your Own Doctor

II

"We Are An Endangered Species."

*"Source Your Power. Be Committed.
Beingness Illuminates Determination."*

"Life Is A Never-Ending Experience."

By

ANNETTE NOONTIL

The Body Is The Barometer Of The Soul II

ISBN 0 646 19721 5

Cover Design by Tracey O'Mara

Printer: McPherson's Printing Group

1st Printing 1994   *2nd Printing 1995*
3rd Printing 1996   *4th Printing 1997*
5th Printing 1998   *6th Printing 1999*
7th Printing 2000   *8th Printing 2000*
9th Printing 2001   *10th Printing 2002*
11th Printing 2003   *12th Printing 2004*
13th Printing 2005   *14th Printing 2006*

A laminated chart 50 cm X 76 cm of all the positive concepts of the bones (included in this book) is available.

Further details can be obtained from the address below.

www.annettenoontil.com

Box 296 Nunawading
Victoria 3131,
Australia

On Thursday 30th June 2005, Annette Noontil moved peacefully on from the earth's plane, to where new light shines. Her sincere, dedicated and fun-loving nature will be sadly missed, but her spirit lives on.

Other books by Annette Noontil:
The Body Is The Barometer Of The Soul (Out of print)
BEINGNESS A commitment to self
One Thousand Petalled Lotus

Distributor - Brumby Books
         10 Southfork Drive
         Kilsyth South
         Victoria, 3137
         Australia

Addendum page 151

CONTENTS

ACKNOWLEDGEMENTS

My special thanks to Peter Munday who laughingly suggested, over a Korean dinner in Brisbane, during Expo '88, that I could name my next book, "The Car Is The Barometer Of Your Direction, So Be Your Own Mechanic." We were talking about when our car "fails to proceed", each part that breaks down has a relationship to our direction. Chapter 19 has his great title and he has given me some clues that I have included.

To Kate Parrott, for offering her husband Graeme's services to type and put this on a word processor and saying "Well -- give it to him **NOW!**"

For you Graeme, I thank you very much for your patience and help with my alterings and additions over a long period.

He even has to type his own "thanks!"

To all my friends who have helped distribute my first book. To the people who have written to me who have found that my concepts for healing your body by changing your thoughts **does work**.

I do appreciate it and I thank you all.

Annette has a major skill. That skill is not writing - though she does that very well. It is not communicating with her Angels - though she does that very well too. Partly, it is the ability to cut through the rubbish and get to the real issue. She sees through all the side issues, all the tangents, all the diversions that get people caught up in when dealing with their own problems. It is what she does next that sets her apart. She clearly defines the solutions.

She can do it because she can step out of her own problems. When she is working with others she is being of service absolutely. She does it without judgement and without conditions. She does it because she loves you. She loves watching problems dissolve - people move closer and closer to their true selves.

That is her skill and it is in this book. This is not a book to just read. It is really not for study either. This is a reference book. It is to be used every day. Whenever any problem arises in your day, use this book. If it is still intact after twelve months, you have been missing out on opportunities to learn about yourself. Use her skill. That is why she is here. Each time you use it, you move closer to your REAL SELF and so does she.

If you have picked up this book, it means that you are somewhere on the same path that I am. It leads to being the best we can be at whatever we came here to do. We simply cannot really do anything else however. It is not an easy path, simple yes, easy no.

You can, if you choose, put this book down, sneak away and pretend that you never picked it up. OR you can take a deep breath, close your eyes and jump into the glorious abyss that is the world of Spirit. If you take that leap you need a safety net. Annette Noontil is mine. You will know right now or will shortly meet yours. There will be no doubt who it is.

When I have been deep in that black pit and lost sight of the light, Annette has been there for me. Sometimes on the phone, sometimes in person. It used to take me days to realize that I needed help. Now I know in seconds. *That's Progress!*

If you have read this far, you are going to take the leap. Congratulations! It is sometimes scary, but when you allow yourself to be fully in the light, the feeling of bliss is beyond description.

To you Annette, bless you. To you reading this, bless you. Though we may never meet in the flesh, we all know and love and support each other. Remember, the path leads to "being the best you can be" and it doesn't get any better than that.

Love to you all.

Andrew Snowdon

INTRODUCTION

I am Annette Noontil and my main aim in life is to make sure of doing everything that is in my power to ensure that as many people will come to understand that **everything we think has an effect on our bodies.**

When I first found this out, my body was about to "throw in the towel." My Guidance had led me to where I found the ability to communicate with them. This was the most exciting experience I had ever had in my life. I wanted to tell all my friends because I wanted them to experience the same joy that I had by knowing I could receive answers to any question I was presuming unanswerable. I simply could not believe that my friends were not interested in talking to their Angels the way I did.

Why we have Spiritual Helpers is to help us learn all the truths that have been hidden from us that has kept us from being the multi-dimensional beings that we need to become.

The understanding of why things in my life needed to change was shown to me whenever I was shown the reasons why I did things. People have different reactions to different situations due to their previous experiences. We all store up our memories and according to our memories, our reactions will appear.

To cope with life in the present time, these reactions need to be understood so that they can be seen as learning experiences, not limitations or fears.

When I regroup a situation, I learn from it and can move on without holding a grudge or blaming someone else. I have learned to be thankful and grateful for my experiences - traumatic or pleasant as the case may be.

This is the healing that I discovered to be the easiest and simplest form. Once I started to change my thoughts, my body responded and my life became interesting. I began working out the corresponding workings of our organs to the way we react with our thoughts.

The difference between my life now is that I see my body as a vehicle to learn from, not a vehicle to use for sickness.

You all have an inner essence to draw on. When you bring forth this essence you feel able to face whatever life experience you need to have. I attract what I need to learn. My growth has come from always asking what I learned from a situation and why I had it. Trusting that there is always a solution to everything.

This is trusting yourself and taking charge of your thinking which is what this book is all about. I have sourced my inner essence. To have this knowledge is very frustrating when I am wanting to give it out all the time. The majority of people cannot believe it or will not believe it. That does not deter me any more. I know that I am my own healer and I am the one in control of my life.

My cold hands and cold feet are an indication that I am scared to bring forth this information but I know my need is to share it. I cannot hide my light under the proverbial bushell. This information is the light. Ignorance is the dark and we have lived in that for too long now.

Self acceptance was what I needed. I was asked to write five good qualities of mine and the person sitting next to me had to tell me as I could not think of one. I could easily list ten or more bad qualities. It saddens me when I see so many people who are not accepting themselves and are unable to stand up for themselves in the same way.

My self acceptance now, allows me to say "NO!" without a twinge of guilt or worry what other people think if that is how I feel. I do not have to agree with people to be accepted by them any more. Being accepted by myself is what really matters.

My wish is that this book will help you gain understanding of how simple it is to heal your body by changing your thoughts.

There is an urgency to achieve this before the year 2000, which is just over five years away.

In every aspect of life there are changes. Old rules no longer work. Structure is limitation. As your understanding increases, you will no longer expect things to be the same as they were. Your creativity will be required to keep you open and growing. Follow your wisdom within. You all receive inner knowings - **use THEM!**

There is a common human failing, that we perceive what a thing is worth by the dollars we pay for it. All this Spiritual information is free. It is only a person's time we are paying for and people will continue to be charged a high price for it until we realize we have it inside of us.

With my first book, I went to the trouble of paying a copyright fee of $100. I have since come to the conclusion that nobody owns anything. (Remember, possessiveness will keep you earthbound!).

This book contains understanding that I have brought forth and what has been brought forth to me, either by someone telling me or by me reading it or by my payment to somebody to teach it to me. It is my need to pass on this information to others. Everything has been said before at some time and my thanks go to all the people who have given their knowledge out to the world in some form to be passed on. If you wait until you are perfect before you share your wisdom, people will be dead! Be married to the process of looking inside for your answers and giving it out and be divorced from the result -- what people do with your information is none of your business.

Hopefully, this information may make a difference to your lives as it most certainly has done to mine.

Welcome to this "Updated Version" of my book.

With Love, Light and Laughter,

Annette.

CHAPTER 1

"THE NEED TO LOOK INSIDE"

This book is for you to look into yourselves when you have an ailment of any kind. A lot of people do not want to do that. They can see faults in others, but they do not realize that they cannot see it in others unless they have it in themselves. So if anyone says something derogatory about you, you can say, "It takes one to know one!"

This notion has been my quickest way to find out what I need to change because what I see in others, I have in myself. It also works when I see something really positive in a person, I know I have it in me so I can then feel good about myself.

Must you wait until you are desperate or nearly dying before you take a look at what you are doing to yourself.

If you take a look and work out what you are doing to cause a small ailment, then it could stop a big ailment building up in the future.

When you read what causes your trouble, do not say, "I don't do that" ask your inner self and then you will see how you do it. Everyone is unique, so the generalization is there for you to go by. Then see how your unique way has created your ailment. The next question is, "How can I change that?" Then ask for some help to do it. *(See "The Need to Change" Chapter.)*

I am just getting you to look at everything with open eyes. Humans are here to Reason and manage this planet. When you reason out why you do the things you do and change for your own good, the planet will be managed properly as you would like it to be.

THE CONSCIOUS THOUGHTS OF THE BODIES ON THIS PLANET OVERSEE THE ENERGY OF THIS SOLAR SYSTEM
(See Chapter 3)

We have free will on this planet so you do not have to change if you want to keep suffering. If you want to change and heal your body, use this book to see what you need to change in your thinking.

This is a do it yourself book. You have all your answers inside you for your life. Your life needs to be a do it yourself life. No one else can live it for you. No one else can breathe for you. No one else can eat for you. No one else can raise your level of consciousness. The only thing you **have** to do in this life is to be responsible for yourself -- and **your body is the barometer** that tells you when you are not. If you are not doing for yourself, your body will be sick and suffering pain.

"Peace Comes From Being In Control Of Your Own Life"

Disease does not bring pain. The pain of your soul brings disease. Pain is good because it gives you the idea that you need to look into yourself. Use the pain.

Understand that you are a soul with a physical body (not a physical body with a soul) a spiritual being - energy - and that soul is the energy or the life force that keeps the cells of your body alive. If you are having trouble with your body, you need to go to your soul and see where you are going against your soul's plan this lifetime. By changing that concept or the way you are thinking, your body will heal. In fact, if you are having trouble with your loved ones or your friends, your soul part is where you go to heal it.

This is how we grow spiritually and raise our level of consciousness to become one with all. This is the reason for coming to this planet, to heal ourselves of limitations and fears. These fears etc., stop us from experiencing the way we can use our skills and our full potential to manage the planet's resources responsibly; but our judgement of self and others cause these fears to suppress our expressions of joy.

Fear is a false god, and you do not need it. Become fearless. Have faith in yourself. Love yourself. Do not be afraid to look inside. I recall seeing a television programme about Eskimos, who were sensitive to their environment. They understood how to look after it while doing for themselves. Then the Canadians came with their radios, televisions and material things and wanted furs and more furs.

These material things that the white man had, **started the Eskimos thinking that they were INFERIOR.** So they worked at killing all the animals to sell the furs so they could have the radios and television sets -- I think you know the rest -- Now they have forgotten their knowledge about caring for their environment and they sit around watching their television and waiting for their dole cheques to come. Their young people are spending their time at discos and taking drugs. No doubt there are not many animals left to use for their own benefit.

Can you see that it was that **one** thought that they were **inferior** that made them lose their self-esteem. When you lose **faith in yourself** the doubting begins and the fears move right in. You only have yourself to blame, as you are the one who let it happen.

We are only using our potential to approximately 8% at the most. What are we doing with that 92%? Delve deeper inside for those answers for what you can do for yourself. Find what you are good at, and what you enjoy doing, and go do it. You did not come here to suffer. There is always a solution, if you only look inside. It is the solving of this solution which is important to you.

"We Are What We Repeatedly Do. Excellence Then,
Is Not An Act, But A Habit"

A lot of us live by other people's standards, for the simple reason that we choose our parents to give us a body so we can learn and grow here on planet earth. We hope these parents will teach us to rid ourselves of some old habits but during our formative years from birth to seven years, we take in everything that our parents do or say. Therefore, we add some of their bad habits and so it goes on.

Some of these standards we have from our parents we do not need -- Some of us need a "Parentectomy"!! If we do not realize we are living by other people's standards, we start putting these standards on to others. Then we put harsh standards on to ourselves. This practice can put you down. Remember, you are No 1 and you are the most important person to you.

All these things that go against us and create disharmony in our thinking are **EMOTIONS -- which are REACTIONS** and they are the way society has taught us to react to things. What other people tell us we ought or should do. It is our intellect, our ego -- our thinking mind and it likes to overtake us. It wants to control our life, but we need to police our thoughts so it cannot take control. The intellect is there **just** to understand your feelings and work out the what, when, where and why of your true feelings, and do it. Not to talk you out of doing things by it's total control of you. Act only on your true feelings. **FEELINGS -- are for ACTION.**

When you follow your true feelings, you are doing what is best for you and you are in control of your own life. Minding your own business and remember that your business is your life. Therefore your life is your business.

Tradition is not always best for you. Do not follow blindly what you have been taught. If you wander off your path or just waste your life on trivia, you know innately that there was a "sign post" at the beginning that told you. You simply forgot to discern it or you did not want to take notice of it before you went on that "off" route. Listen for the signs from your feelings before drifting off. Use your feelings always. It is how you feel that is important. Look inside for what is right for you. Learn to be flexible. Always know why you do the things you do. If it is not applicable to you in this century -- give it up. You do not need it. -- Change and grow. -- Do not be held back by other people's judgement if you want to change. If you are worrying about what other people are thinking about you, you are not minding your own business.

This misplaced importance on little things creates pressure. These pressures can be guilt, fear, worry, anger, yearning, hatred or jealousy. All these concepts cause ailments to your body because they are all keeping you from loving yourself. If you take a look at your body and see anything that has just occurred, such as a pimple, a knock, a cut or a mosquito bite, it needs to be looked into because nothing is a co-incidence.

"Know Yourself To Feel Sure Of Yourself"

Look up the Bones Concepts Chapter, and whatever bone it is near, look inside yourself to see why you are not living that positive concept. Anything that is stopping you from loving yourself will eventually cause an ailment in your body. Therefore, that is the reason **you need to learn from your body ailments** and understand what you have let happen to yourself by having that negative thought.

Thoughts are energy and they are powerful.

Use this power to work for you, not against you, by changing your thoughts to heal your body. The pressure that an illness can give you can be termed "good" because you will be forced to do something for yourself and change and learn from it. Some so called incurable diseases can be cured by simply changing the thoughts that have caused it because the cells of your body completely rejuvenate each seven years as you go into a new learning cycle. -- It may take time, but you **can** heal your body if you want to. There are a few people who do not want to change and heal their bodies. -- They will just need to do it next lifetime.

If you keep the big picture of you as a soul needing to keep evolving and learning from everything you do, you will not waste your time while here this lifetime.

Tiffs between loved ones or quarrels with anyone, are simply to take a look at yourself to see why you **react** in a certain way. If you do not do something about these reactions, your body will soon tell you with an ache or pain etc. Impatience could be a reaction that stops you from understanding. Change and get back to your feelings, before your body is affected from having these altercations with anyone.

Get on with looking inside you to know yourself and understand why you do the things you do. Why do you limit yourself with fears or anything that stops you from being one with all things. -- With all these wars going on inside us, what hope is there to not have wars in our families and to not have global wars? We are such a fearful society. Fear of death gives you a fear of living. Fear of success. Fear of failure. Fear of being found out. Fear of what will people think. -- Who cares really? -- It is how you care about yourself that matters. Nothing is a big deal to you anymore when you accept yourself as you are. When you lose that one with all feeling you have separation. Separation leads to competition and competition is thoughts that you are either greater or lesser than another person. Then you cannot accept yourself and that is where fears come in.

Why have a fear of death, when a soul never dies? A soul is energy, it was, it is, and it always will be. A soul enjoys life when it keeps evolving. We need continuous growth from learning about ourselves. It is the spiritual understanding of what we are doing in the physical that gives us balance.

"The Only Separation You Have Is What You Think You Have"

The left side of your body has to do with your spiritual feelings and the right side of your body has to do with your physical and material thinking.

How do I feel about myself? Why do I get emotional over a small incident? What has given me a fear of heights? It is questions like these that help you to help yourself grow spiritually and to raise your level of consciousness. Why put up with limitations? Everything can be solved by understanding yourself.

From here, you begin to put yourself first and you grow in leaps and bounds. Things start falling into place, doors are opening for you, miracles happen. When you put yourself first and do for yourself, you will not get sick. When you are sick you have to have someone to look after you. Now -- is it selfish to put yourself first??? You are no use to others when you are sick which is often because you have used all your energy on doing for others, when they could have been doing for themselves. If you have to do for others, make sure you learn something for yourself from what you have done and then you will not be drained.

We feel good when we do or give to others. We love to be of service but nobody loves being a servant. We enjoy giving when we give without expecting anything in return. It is a need of ours to **give** of our love but it is also a need to **take** for ourselves because the more we take, the more we can give. We can not help others unless we have helped ourself first. As always, there needs to be a balance in everything we do. Balance and harmony comes from knowing when to do for ourself and when to do for others. That means we are in harmony when our timing is right and when we are working from our inner feelings and not from what other people tell us or what other people think we should do.

When you are relaxed and at one with yourself, you have your enthusiasm to work in your own timing.

It is your absolute need to look inside and find your purpose and know where you came from, what you are doing here and where you are going, then move into fulfilling your purpose and not waste your time here.

Knowing your direction keeps you living in the present. Forget about being guilty of your past and stop worrying about your future. All you need is to live in the "NOW" and just "BE" yourself.. "BEINGNESS" is your key to your freedom and your one with all-ness.

Self awareness directs you to mind your own business. You are then too busy getting on with your own life to be interfering with other peoples' who in turn could be doing the same. What a wonderful world it would be then.

When you are helping yourself first, that is when you are helping your world.

"It Is Your Attitude, Not Your Aptitude, That Determines Your Altitude"

5

To sum up, the following is my understanding of the reasons to look inside so you can grow spiritually and raise your level of consciousness.

- Becoming enlightened about who you really are, where you came from and what you are doing here and where you are going and finding your purpose.

- Learning from everything you do.

- Healing limitations, fears and thoughts of guilt and suffering, so you can enjoy life.

- Being in control of your own energy and using your time wisely and not wasting it on trivia.

- Minding your own business and not controlling others.

- Developing a "live and let live" attitude or better still a "love and let live" attitude.

- Having a balance between your spiritual life and your physical and material life.

- Understanding yourself and removing any reactions you have been taught that stop you from being the free soul that you are.

- Getting back to being yourself into your true feelings. Not letting your intellect or ego take over your life.

- Being at one with the universe and generally raising your level of consciousness.

"The Spiritual Journey Consists Of Simply Ceasing
To Be An Enemy Of Ourselves"

If your ailment is not included in this book, find out what organ is giving you the problem and just what is the function of that organ. Then see how it corresponds to your thinking. Note which area it is in so you know which chakra it is associated . *(See Chakra Diagram)* Read the introduction to that chakra to know the best way to be thinking to heal yourself.

To see how the alimentary canal or digestive system corresponds to the way you think, here is the big picture:-
When you take **food** into your mouth you **chew** it with your teeth then swallow it. (that corresponds to having a **plan** and thinking it over and **deciding** to do it) and it goes down to your stomach and it is **digested**. (the equivalent here is **understanding** the plan for yourself because all that is for your PERSONAL area). then you complete the digestion in your small intestine. (this is your BUSINESS area where the deal or plan is completed) then to your large intestine where the final extraction of moisture takes place and the food residue is excreted. (that represents your SOCIAL area where you take what you want for yourself and then outflow what you want to give to others.

Can you see your need to be solid in your understanding in your PERSONAL to cope with your BUSINESS and SOCIAL areas of your life?

I heard the hostages who were held in Iran saying that they had teeth problems. The reason being that they could only make plans which they chewed over and chewed over and chewed over. They could not do anything with their plans because they were chained to a wall. (That was forced procrastination!)

"Injustices Are Just Obstacles For You To Get Around And Disregard"

CHAPTER 2

"THE POSITIVE CONCEPTS OF THE BONES
TO KEEP THEM HEALTHY AND THE CHAKRA
THAT GOVERNS EACH BONE"

All the diagrams and concepts in this chapter can be obtained on a laminated wall chart. *(See page II for details)*

It shows you that every bone has a positive concept to keep it healthy. The same as every organ in our body has it's own positive concept.

In the chapters following this one, I have described the seven energy centres, called chakras. Each one is for a different learning experience and governs different areas of the body.

Beside the concept of each bone, there is a coloured square with the number of the chakra in it. This tells you that this bone is governed by a certain chakra. Read the introduction to the relevant chakra to see what overall concept you need to be living as well as the positive concept of the bone.

You use these positive concepts of the bones, depending on whether your ailment is a bone, a muscle, a tendon, a ligament, a nerve or the skin over the bone. Read the "How to use this Chart" and you will see that if your trouble is a bone, it is resentment causing you to not live that positive concept. If it is any of the others, they have a different reason for stopping you.

The next thing to take note of is whether your affliction is on your left side or right side. Your left side is to do with your Spiritual life. Your right side is your Physical or Material life.

Your arms are to do with **doing** and your legs are your **direction**.

Each finger has an overall concept of it's own and is stated on the heading of each finger.

The toes are different, the concept goes across each type of bone and is listed underneath the diagram.

You can use these concepts to help you see what you need to change if you only have a bump, a bruise or a burn, etc. because these are early warning signals for you to look into. Nip them in the bud so you do not have bigger problems later on.

The concept of each intervertebral **disc** is BELONGING.

"Orthodox Medicine Used To Be Alternative Medicine."

*CHAKRAS – ENERGY CENTRES

1. PINEAL – Inflow – Self Acceptance – Patience
2. COCCYX – Wants – Loyalty to Self
3. REPRODUCTIVE – Needs – One with All (No Competition)
4. SOLAR PLEXUS – Identity – Positivity
5. HEART – Drive – Devotion to Self
6. THYROID – Relating – Compassion (No Judging)
7. PITUITARY – Outflow – Humility (No Glory)

HOW TO USE THIS CHART

The positive concepts are for you to know how you need to think to keep you healthy. Whatever you have wrong with you, pinpoint the bone it is near and use below** concepts that effect it, such as – If you have trouble in a **muscle**, your **guilt** stops you from living the positive concept of the bone that is near this muscle.

Note: Also which Chakra governs the area of the bone and refer to the overall concept of the Chakras above*.

** Bones = Resentment   Nerves = Unbalanced Communication
   Ligaments = Control   Skin = Unworthy/Inadequate
   Muscles = Guilt   Tendons = Inflexibility

For ailments and more understanding of each Chakra refer to the book
"THE BODY IS THE BAROMETER OF THE SOUL – So Be Your Own Doctor"
by Annette Noontil.

SKULL

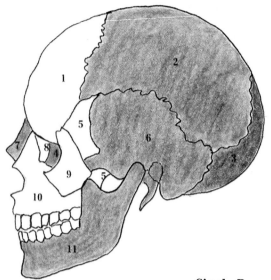

Single Bones

7 1. **Frontal** – Plan outflow, doing develops seeing
– *Seeing what needs to be done.*

6 3. **Occipital** – Relax when relating to everything without any judging.

1 4. **Ethmoid** – Knowledge is growth.

7 5. **Sphenoid** – Visualize your direction of your plan.

1 11. **Mandible** – Acceptance of new things will be understood
– *By chewing over ideas you see the worth of them and whether those ideas are for you to take in.*

1 ◆ **Vomer** – Satisfaction when you learn.

1 ◆ **Hyoid** – Ability to take in information.

Right – Physical

1 2. **Parietal** – Learn to just be when living this life
– *Live the love of your own true feelings which is being yourself without thinking impatient thoughts about yourself.*

1 6. **Temporal** – Use your ears for more information
– *When you are tolerant and open, you are more receptive.*

1 7. **Nasal** – Be open to new things.

7 8. **Lacrimal** – When assessing, see best qualities
– *Always look for good in people and things.*

[7] 9. **Zygomatic** – Relax to see every feeling expressed.

[7] 10. **Maxilla** – Saying what you feel will create a wayshower –
When you share your feelings you are an example to others.

[1] ◆ **Inferior Nasal Concha** – Be inspired when living and growing.

[7] ◆ **Palatine** – Before you speak organize what to say.

MIDDLE EAR

[1] ◆ **Malleus** – Through patience and self acceptance you gain respect.

[1] ◆ **Incus** – Be tolerant of all you do.

[1] ◆ **Stapes** – Insights come when you listen to others.

Left – Spiritual

[1] 2. **Parietal** – Self acceptance for yourself from insights of patience
*– The more understanding you have of yourself the more you will accept
yourself and be patient with yourself.*

[1] 6. **Temporal** – You gain more knowledge because you listen.

[1] 7. **Nasal** – Learning from everything will raise your consciousness.

[7] 8. **Lacrimal** – Living by perceiving enlightened images.

[7] 9. **Zygomatic** – Share your feelings, therefore you grow spiritually
*– When you say what you really mean and feel, you gain respect for
yourself. Trusting what you say from your heart enables you to share what
you know so that you take it in for yourself as well.*

[7] 10. **Maxilla** – Ability to share to gain fulfillment.

[1] ◆ **Inferior Nasal Concha** – Self acceptance of your life.

[7] ◆ **Palatine** – Show your feelings to be sincere.

MIDDLE EAR

[1] ◆ **Malleus** – Your understanding grows when you listen from inside
– Take note of your intuition or the wee small voice from within.

[1] ◆ **Incus** – Be open to learn from everything.

[1] ◆ **Stapes** – Be tolerant of what you hear.

◆ Not illustrated (bones inside head)

THORAX

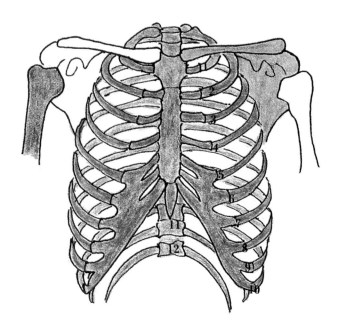

5   **Sternum – Breast**

You must be devoted to self, caring and concerned.

Right – Physical Doing

7   **Scapula – Shoulder**
Taking responsibility of your time, seeing it is directed for your benefit – *What you do with work and involvement, must be to gain from it.*

7   **Clavicle – Collar**
Ability to share your skills so others learn
– *Give of your service so that others will know how.*

Left – Spiritual Doing

4   **Scapula – Shoulder**
You are responsible to do for yourself and know who you are
– *You are the only one who can understand yourself to be yourself.*

4   **Clavicle – Collar**
Grow from everything you do with positivity – *Raise your consciousness through learning from being positive about your experiences.*

Right – Physical

5   1. Keeping solid to organize yourself for achieving.

5   2. Know your achievement is for you.

5   3. Follow through is doing it for you – *You're the one who benefits when you complete a job.*

5   4. Ability to achieve for yourself.

5   5. Knowing your enthusiasm will bring fulfillment.

5   6. To succeed, always make sure you love yourself.

5   7. Inner motivation for working towards your goals – *Your incentive must come from wanting to do it for yourself, so that your goals are working or you.*

5   8. Knowing what to do and how to do it for your success.

5   9. Give impetus to your labour to succeed.

5   10. Inner authority for going after balance – *Determination from within to seek the balance between your physical love of others because of your devotion to self. When you love yourself it is easy to love others.*

5   11. Always be flexible in your doing.

5   12. When doing anything, understanding everything is essential.

Left – Spiritual

5   1. Devotion to self from experiences – *The situations you have in life when you put yourself first are the way you achieve success.*

5   2. Giving and receiving is the balance you require.

5   3. Your growth depends on knowledge gained while you are fulfilled.

5   4. Always trust what understanding gained.

5   5. Through love, achievement for you is easy.

5   6. Willing to proceed experiencing and being determined.

5   7. Always know why you do the things you do.

5   8. Follow your feelings for everything you do.

5   9. Take stock, learning from achievements .

5   10. Trust yourself with your growth.

5   11. Know you have balance when you enjoy
– *Enjoyment comes from loving yourself as much as others.*

5   12. Taking in knowledge helps fulfillment.

SPINE

Cervical

6 1. Atlas – Your life depends on your inner true
     feelings – *Use your true feelings always which are
     what you really feel inside, not how you are
     taught to react or play the games of society and do
     what others think you should do.*

6 2. Axis – Flexibility allows you to be – *Flexibility is
     freedom and ability to change to another way and
     find that you can totally live in the present.*

6 3. Always be comfortable with other people.

6 4. Use the ability of fairness when you relate.

6 5. Show feelings of compassion when interacting.

6 6. You can relax showing others sincerity – *When
     you are sincere and open with how you feel and
     just be yourself, you can relax.*

6 7. Equality in relationships bring about harmony.

Thoracic

5 1. Having direction for yourself gives out peace.

5 2. Always think big to achieve your success.

5 3. Be organised with incentive when doing anything.

5 4. Have inner motivation for your drive – *Your
     motivation for action must come from your own
     feelings, not from others telling you what you
     should or ought to do or because it is the 'done
     thing' or it is tradition. Do it because YOU want to.*

5 5. Keep the big picture while executing task – *While
     working at your task, remember what it will be like
     when it is finished or keep your vision of the
     completed job and why you are doing it.*

5 6. Power comes from devotion to self – *You must put
     yourself No. 1. No one else can give you power, it
     comes from inside you. You lose strength when you
     are devoted to someone or something else.*

5 7. You gain fulfillment when you follow through –
     *After planning a job and working out how to do it, and
     having the drive to complete it is what is fulfilling.*

14

`5` 8. Enjoyment comes when you do for yourself

`5` 9. Know that your love is your energy force
– *When you know you are love, you understand that love is your power.*

`5` 10. Do it your way when performing any work.

`5` 11. Performance through sincerity makes heart your strength
– *Your strength comes from the love in you heart and when you are sincere about loving yourself first, your performance is sincere.*

`5` 12. Be willing to love yourself then everything flows.

Lumbar

`4` 1. Through spiritual and physical growth you reach maturity – *To mature you need to understand that what you do and have in the physical world is what you use to grow spiritually.*

`4` 2. Growth with sincerity in yourself gains wisdom – *When you are sincere with yourself that you really want to raise your level of consciousness, that is when you gain wisdom.*

`4` 3. Your positivity keeps you spiralling upwards – *You raise your level of consciousness by eliminating limitations.*

`4` 4. Your beingness guides energy while knowing yourself – *Your freedom to be yourself is what drives you while looking into yourself.*

`4` 5. Self identity with empathy will enlighten you – *You will grow in consciousness if you have understanding of who you are.*

Sacral

`3` 1. FOOD – Enlightenment gives you your need – *Spiritual growth by understanding everything you do.*

`3` 2. HEALTH – Your vitality is your need.

`3` 3. SHELTER – Secure within yourself is your need to live – *Inner strength and knowledge gives you security within yourself.*

`3` 4. LOVE – Your need is to teach – *Pass on your love by giving forth your knowledge.*

`3` 5. SEX – It is your need to attain oneness – *To be at one with yourself and others without competing.*

Coccyx

`2` 1. Make goals for your basic wants.

`2` 2. Your wants are to gain more awareness.

`2` 3. Your wants are to have abundance for you.

`2` 4. Your wants are to understand you experiences.

ARMS

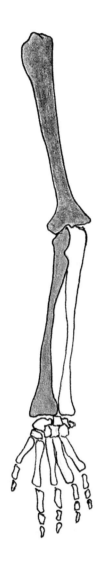

Right – Physical Doing

6 **Humerus** – Compassion when you relate to others to support them – *Let others be themselves when guiding them towards their beingness.*

4 **Radius** – Be an individual when raising your ability to achieve – *Understand why you are beginning to accomplish for yourself.*

7 **Ulna** – Moving towards giving your time to others so that you learn for yourself – *By sharing what you know or do, you gain knowledge from your doing.*

Carpals – Wrist (Up and Down)

7 1. **Scaphoid** – Move up or down as a wayshower – *Being an example to others in whatever emotion is manifesting.*

4 2. **Lunate** – To raise or lower your empathy on being – *You need balance when showing understanding of your feelings.*

5 3. **Triquetrum** – Devotion to self creates loving your doing.

2 4. **Pisiform** – Do more or less goals.

(Sideways)

3 5. **Trapezium** – Outwards with no competition – *When going out to obtain your needs, be at one with everyone.*

6 6. **Trapezoid** – Expand while relating – *When talking to others your mind grows.*

4 7. **Capitate** – Knowing you are love when being in an outgoing situation – *Understanding yourself so you are secure while doing every outward circumstance intended.*

7 8. **Hamate** – Be outgoing in your sharing.

HANDS

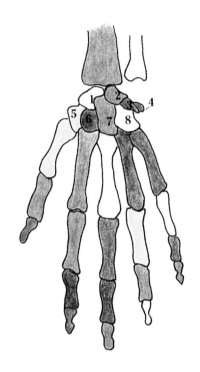

Right – Physical Doing

Thumb – Flexibility

2 **Distal** – Be flexible in how you create your physical goals.

4 **Proximal** – Listen to your feelings to be flexible.

3 **Metacarpal** – Be flexible and creative to hold on to your needs.

First Finger – Direction from your intellect

5 **Distal** – Follow your direction in the way you want to go.

6 **Middle** – Follow your direction with compassion – *What you do, needs to have consideration shown to all.*

4 **Proximal** – Follow your direction with positivity – *You must know where you are going and why.*

2 **Metacarpal** – Be directed to grasp what you want.

Second Finger – Common Sense

4 **Distal** – Doing things with positivity is sensible.

6 **Middle** – Doing things with compassion is sensible – *You can enjoy working when it is with love always being your motive.*

5 **Proximal** – Doing things the way you want to do them is sensible.

7 **Metacarpal** – Practical application of energy released to hold on for myself to be able to pass it on – *Knowing how to do things to understand for yourself to give it out.*

Third Finger – Feelings

7 **Distal** – Doing things for others without expecting in return.

4 **Middle** – Positive creativity to move on – *Successful achievement growing through knowing yourself.*

3 **Proximal** – Creative doing is a need.

6 **Metacarpal** – Relate to your feelings while taking a hold on anything – *Feelings are all that matter so you can understand experiences easily for yourself.*

Fourth Finger – Ability to Communicate

4 **Distal** – Positive Communication – *Have more self awareness.*

5 **Middle** – Communicate the way you want to – *Show your love with your own creativity.*

7 **Proximal** – Giving out creative speech – *Sharing your feelings humbly, sensitively spoken.*

5 **Metacarpal** – Speaking what you want to say to hold respect for self.

17

ARMS

Left – Spiritual Doing

[7] **Humerus** – Learn from giving your time to support others – *You support yourself when you learn from giving and supporting others.*

[6] **Radius** – No judgement as you raise yourself to relate to yourself – *Do not put yourself down or feel guilty at what you have done before. Everything you do is to learn from so you can know yourself.*

[5] **Ulna** – When spiralling upwards, do it your way – *When raising your level of consciousness, you are the only one who makes the decisions.*

Carpals – Wrist (Up and Down)

[6] 1. **Scaphoid** – Being one with all when relating.

[3] 2. **Lunate** – Raise or lower your strength to obtain your needs.

[5] 3. **Triquetrum** – Too much outside devotion or too little devotion to self.

[7] 4. **Pisiform** – More or less giving.

(Sideways)

[2] 5. **Trapezium** – Have broader goals.

[7] 6. **Trapezoid** – Give out your sharing.

[4] 7. **Capitate** – By expanding your knowledge you shall know who you are.

[6] 8. **Hamate** – For outward direction, no judgement of self or others.

HANDS

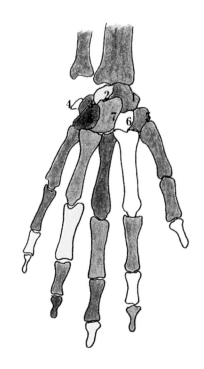

Left – Spiritual Doing

Thumb – Flexibility
| 7 | **Distal** – be flexible when sharing your spiritual wisdom.

| 5 | **Proximal** – Have flexibility and enthusiasm for your desires.

| 5 | **Metacarpal** – Be flexible when learning for yourself.

First Finger – Direction from your intellect
| 4 | **Distal** – Do positively with all the facts.

| 7 | **Middle** – Be factually organized with your direction.

| 2 | **Proximal** – Learn from doing you goals for your direction.

| 7 | **Metacarpal** – Be directed to share your knowledge so you take in more for yourself.

Second Finger – Common Sense
| 3 | **Distal** – Using your wisdom to gain your needs – *Your understanding will produce your food, health, shelter, love and sex.*

| 5 | **Middle** – Using your own solutions makes you happy.

| 4 | **Proximal** – Respect your own positive creative solution.

| 6 | **Metacarpal** – Use good judgement to relate to what you hold on to.

Third Finger – Feelings
| 6 | **Distal** – Being creative with compassion for all things – *Use your own inspiration and have a live and let live feeling for everything.*

| 2 | **Middle** – Believing in your own creativity – *Your loyalty to yourself enables you to know the strength you have.*

| 3 | **Proximal** – Being sincere when creating you own solutions – *When it is your need, your answers work for you.*

| 4 | **Metacarpal** – Love thoughts while showing empathy for self when you learn – *Your growth is knowing how to feel your love.*

Fourth Finger – Ability to Communicate
| 7 | **Distal** – Organizing your sharing creativity.

| 3 | **Middle** – A need to create learning and teaching – *You grow from doing for self to help others.*

| 5 | **Proximal** – Use your own wisdom to communicate your creativity.

| 2 | **Metacarpal** – You need to communicate to have loyalty to yourself – *By knowing what you want you can tell people what you want.*

19

HIP – Ilium – Ischium – Pubis

Right – Physical
3 You need to energize life – *Keep learning new things to have interest and stimulation of your energy.*

Left – Spiritual
3 Keep enlightened is your need – *Strive always to raise your level of consciousness.*

LEGS

Right – Physical Direction

3 **Femur – Thigh** – Determination to obtain your needs.

4 **Patella – Knee** – Learning from everything you do – *Transforming your awareness.*

5 **Tibia – Shin** – Directing yourself to do it your way.

7 **Fibula – Calf** – Telling yourself to give your time – *Use your time wisely for yourself.*

Tarsus – Ankle

7 1. **Calcaneus – Heel** – Visualize the reality of your direction always.

7 2. **Talus** – When you have a skill share it – *When you have mastered something, practise it.*

7 3. **Navicular** – When you organize your path it flows – *Know where you are going and how you plan to do it and you will run to time.*

7 4. **Cuboid** – You need to be a wayshower – *You must need to be an example.*

7 5. **Cuneiform – Lateral** – Give the time to share – *Take time to give of yourself with either skills or knowledge.*

7 6. **Cuneiform – Intermediate** – Your knowledge is for sharing – *When you know something, tell it to anyone who might like to know it.*

7 7. **Cuneiform – Medial** – Share your abundance with feeling – *When you give of yourself, do it with love.*

FEET

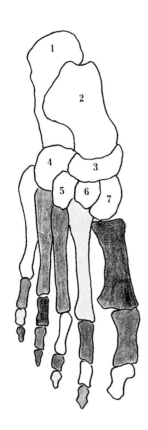

Toes

Distal = Balance
Middle = Support
Proximal = Regulate
Metatarsals = Control

Right – Physical Direction

Big Toe

7 | **Distal** – Your timing is essential for level management.

5 | **Proximal** – Inner authority to love yourself.

6 | **Metatarsal** – Have the will to stop judging yourself or others.

First Toe

4 | **Distal** – Moving on with positive identity – *Your direction is good when you trust who you are, where you came from, what you are doing here and where you are going.*

7 | **Middle** – Use your will power to be organized.

5 | **Proximal** – Discipline is required to do for self.

3 | **Metatarsal** – Have control when no competition – *When you feel no greater or no lesser than others, your control of yourself is your business.*

Second Toe

3 | **Distal** – Going forward with no competition is the way.

2 | **Middle** – Determination will keep you loyal to yourself – *Inner strength to follow your desires.*

7 | **Proximal** – Regulate your outflow to be of service – *Make sure that your outflow is of service to yourself as well as others.*

5 | **Metatarsal** – You are in charge when you do it your way.

Third Toe

5 | **Distal** – Go ahead when doing for yourself.

4 | **Middle** – You must persevere with positive feelings – *Always keep understanding why you do the things you learn from.*

6 | **Proximal** – Adjust your mind to have no judgement – *A live and let live attitude is what will change your thoughts of others.*

2 | **Metatarsal** – Know what you want for yourself.

Fourth Toe

2 | **Distal** – Having future goals assist your onward path.

3 | **Middle** – You must have responsibility for your needs – *You are the one who must take the initiative for what you need.*

4 | **Proximal** – Become steady by assuring time for yourself – *Regulate your direction so that you have time to do for yourself.*

7 | **Metatarsal** – Direct yourself to seeing what to say – *Control yourself to be either passive or aggressive in every situation.*

21

LEGS

Left – Spiritual Direction

7　**Femur – Thigh** – Have inner strength to be of service.

6　**Patella – Knee** – Rigidity stops relating, so bend.

4　**Tibia – Shin** – Showing the way to be yourself – *Telling your intellect to listen to your true feelings and be the way you feel.*

5　**Fibula – Calf** – Love is what guides you into fulfillment.

Tarsus – Ankle

5　1. **Calcaneus – Heel** – To follow through, you do for yourself.

5　2. **Talus** – To go forward, you need incentive.

5　3. **Navicular** – Do it your way for achievement.

5　4. **Cuboid** – Forward with respect for yourself.

5　5. **Cuneiform – Lateral** – Show your love with action – *You are energy and that energy is love. Let it be seen when you are doing.*

5　6. **Cuneiform – Intermediate** – Use your love and move on to oneness – *When you are being your love, you can be at one with all things.*

5　7. **Cuneiform – Medial** – Be the love that you are.

FEET

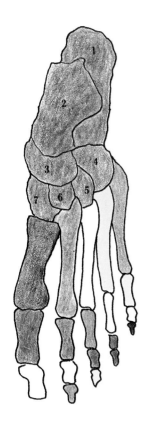

Left – Spiritual Direction

Big Toe

7 **Distal** – Balance your life by sharing always from your true feelings.

5 **Proximal** – Know that you can support yourself with devotion – *You back yourself by being devoted to yourself first.*

6 **Metatarsal** – See that relating is through compassion – *When dealing with others, have a live and let live attitude and that is caring for self a well.*

First Toe

4 **Distal** – Know your direction and never sway from it.

7 **Middle** – The path to take is willingness to share.

5 **Proximal** – Make sure you do it your way.

2 **Metatarsal** – Be sure to go after your goals.

Second Toe

3 **Distal** – Oneness needs no competition raising one's consciousness – *To spiritually grow in consciousness, you need to be at one with yourself and others.*

2 **Middle** – Always have loyalty to plan goals – *You came to earth to be loyal to yourself, so you need to plan goals to achieve for yourself.*

4 **Proximal** – Manage your empathy to have time for self – *It is a must for you to have personal time for yourself.*

7 **Metatarsal** – Use inner authority to organize your path – *Your direction needs to have control from within when working it out.*

Third Toe

2 **Distal** – Your loyalty to yourself will gain your achievement – *To achieve any goal at all, your first thought is to spiritually achieve at the same time.*

5 **Middle** – Devotion to self is your first responsibility.

7 **Proximal** – Give of your time to impart your knowledge.

3 **Metatarsal** – Your basic needs are to respect yourself.

Fourth Toe

6 **Distal** – With compassion for self and others always.

7 **Middle** – Be aware of your organization of facts.

3 **Proximal** – You grow and mature through oneness.

4 **Metatarsal** – Make yourself positive towards yourself.

23

CHAPTER 3

"THE CONSCIOUS THOUGHTS OF THE BODIES ON THIS PLANET OVERSEE THE ENERGY OF THIS SOLAR SYSTEM"

By that statement above, you can see that we all need to get our acts together and police our thoughts to be in control of ourselves and be what our inner feelings want for us. Just look at one news session on the television and anyone could see that our planet is in a bad state. Murder, violence, rape, drug taking, harsh treatment of domestic animals, (and we ingest those emotions of those ill treated animals), annihilation of our rain forests, (making indigenous people and wild animals homeless), spraying chemicals on our food, pollution of our waters, oil spills, nuclear and radio active pollution, wars, wasting resources and total disregard for anything but material gain.

You would think we would have had enough of all that by now. It seems to be far easier to embrace all those negative thoughts rather than to love ourselves and to have harmony in our families and be tolerant of our neighbours and understand different cultures and be at one with nations.

The quality of our life depends on the quality of our thinking and our thinking has overtaken our feelings.

Everybody on earth today is responsible for the state of the planet and for the situation they are in.

To change the world, you must change yourself first.

To help the world, you must help yourself first.

To understand the world, you must understand yourself first.

The way we keep being controlled by material possessions, power hungry behaviour and most of all being **judgmental** and give not a thought to our spiritual nature and the reasons we are here on this planet, we are headed for the same fate as Atlantis.

If we all had the quality of our lives as our first priority, the earth would not need to make the changes that it is making at present, such as clearing the planet of people by earthquakes etc. The earth is a living organism and it is about to assert itself and free itself of people who do not love themselves. They judge themselves and everything, therefore they do not respect earth. When people are not in their feelings and only working from their intellects, the earth becomes brittle. This being the reason for floods to soften the earth and people feel for others during the flood but when the water subsides, they go back to their intellects, bitching that the insurance will not pay, etc. etc. Always blaming someone or something else.

"Facts Do Not Cease To Exist Because They Are Ignored"
- Aldous Huxley

25

We have less than twenty years to wake up to ourselves and stop all this judging of ourselves and judging of others. Also, we must grow and progress above the penis consciousness that has been dominating the human male for thousands of years and the subservient female not being able to speak up for herself.

The time has come now to listen to our inner longing to be free of all outside control and be at one with ourselves and with every level of consciousness from minerals up through to the Prime Creator.

Know that everything is **you**. We are one. Everything that you see around you is **you**. Why do we want to hurt **ourself**, instead of loving ourself?

Does this understanding help you to see what your thoughts are doing to the world? All our weather is a result of our thoughts.

We did not start off with this destructive attitude and neither did Atlantis. We were all powerful, loving, knowledgeable beings. The intention of our planet was to be for other galaxies to exchange information with us, but some creator gods (small "g") fought for ownership of this planet and won and they have blocked us off from that exchange. For thousands of years we have been kept in the dark (ignorant) by taking most of the energy from us. We have existed on very low states of consciousness in comparison with what is our rightful amount. For example, 2 strands of DNA (Deoxyribonucleic acid) instead of 12 strands.

These gods cause chaos and confusion and they thrive on that consciousness. They have kept us separated from ourselves of whom we really are and from other planets and galaxies.

We must cut the frequency link with these creator gods so that we are not controlled by them. Tune into our own consciousness frequency so we can let in the light of the Prime Creator, the Family of Light and other consciousnesses that can enlighten us with their knowledge and information. **Light is information**. Become en-light-ened.

Because we are permanent atom beings we carry our inner essence of love and goodness deep inside always. Therefore we are always saying we want peace but this outside negativity of guilt, fear and blaming etc. has overtaken us and we have forgotten our true reality.

Do you really want to help this planet? If you do, it is best not to get your knickers in a knot over what others are doing to it because that way you are losing your energy and that is what the creator gods are wanting. That is the way they will keep feeding from your energy.

"There Is No Such Thing As Karma. There Is Never A Debt To Pay.
There Is A Divinity To Be"

- Saint Germain

Hate and anger creates a problem for the universe. If you wish to take responsibility for the planet, it would be best done in your meditations. You may not see the result straight away but your thoughts have power.

Especially if twelve people focus on a certain objective there is nothing that cannot be achieved.

Have thirty six people with one mind focussed together and the entire world, even the universe, may be changed.

This can be a thought to help the endangered species - not only our animals, but human species - such as the Tibetans and the indiginous people in Sarawak having their rain forest home removed just for greed.

When we permit extinction through deliberate elimination, we are allowing the opposition to take a stronger hold.

Remember that it is your thoughts that have made the world what it is today. Do not be afraid of change. Trust yourself and acknowledge your greatness and your divinity. Use your power to demand your full potential from understanding who you are. You have a choice to stand up and be counted and speak out what you know to help the ones who are still asleep to this awareness.

That can only happen if we want it and will it and intend it to happen. Our spirituality has simply gone by the wayside. Until we become our spiritual selves and live the love that we are, the good things that happen to us are always overshadowed by one little mishap. The same with our good qualities, we forget about them and only concentrate on what we lack. Comparing ourselves with others instead of coming together as a team and all using what we have in combination to achieve our aims.

That seldom happens in teamwork. If one excels over another we have to start bitching and bullying and cut down the tall poppy.

Everyone of us has different strengths that we have mastered and if we do not use them we will lose them. We need also, to teach our skills and our "know how" to others. Then we can learn new things. Do not expect to learn things instantly. Mastery takes time and practise with patience.

Communication of what we know in team work of peoples coming together and combining our skills for the betterment of the whole, is the synergy we need.

We have all the energy of the sun and the wind and we are not using it. Instead, we pollute the planet with uranium waste and use up all the planet's fossil fuel which alters the structure of the planet. Surely this is stupid. Governments and business must be controlled to do what the people want for the good of the whole planet.

"Every Belief That I Change Increases My Use Of My Own Power"

Know that we need to ask for what we want always and for things to happen. If we do not know what we want, nothing is achieved.

Red Indians made a time to find their "vision quest" that is, they have a vision of their purpose in life and they made a shield of it to remind them and also to let others of their people know what that purpose was.

That is having direction in life. Spiritual direction not materialistic direction. A lot of people do not give a thought to what life is all about, they are too busy going after money and possessions.

Everybody has a purpose. Look inside yourself, find out how you need to grow spiritually. (Page 6 has 10 concepts. Which one needs your attention?)

The creator gods want us to keep being fearful and judgemental. These limitations keep us negative and out of balance with a lack of inner authority and never knowing who we are.

When there is a **full moon** we get both a full charge of negativity from the moon and also a full charge of positivity from the sun because it is fully reflected off the moon. Negative people are charged with even more negativity at this time and it accentuates their own negativity. They do not realize that their negativity attracts more negativity so their situation gets out of hand. This is where the word "lunatic" comes from.

Because these people have been taught their negative thoughts very early, they do not realize there is another way. They only know that way and the worse they become.

This lack of inner authority to be positive allows thoughts from earthbound souls to take them over. They become a trouble to themselves and to everybody else.

Your **EXISTENCE** on this planet has these 7 guidelines to follow:-

KNOW WHO YOU ARE - this is essential to you because you will have direction and purpose for why you are here to have the **feeling that you belong**.

ONE WITH ALL - this is the feeling that you know you are one. One with all nature, minerals, plants and animals. One with all humanity, one with the universe, one with yourself. Respect and love for the other, no matter how different, **they are all you.**

LOVE OF SELF - this is knowing that you are love and you are a powerful energy force radiating that love from your aura. By loving yourself first, your glow attracts others to you and they learn from your example.

"Inner Authority Gets Things Done."

COMMUNICATION - this can be done verbally or non verbally. Speaking our truths and listening to others, brings about our learning. It is giving and receiving. Sharing our feelings. Communication with your inner Guidance is essential for you to understand your experiences and to understand others to communicate with humility.

CREATION - this is bringing forth new ideas which are never ending. There is always another or better way to do something. Know you can create your own destiny by your desire to manifest the best for you. You are the one who can decide what sort of life you want for yourself.

DIRECTION - this is knowing your purpose for being here. When you know this, you make the best decisions for you and you take little notice of fears and limitations that could stop your **Soul's plan.**

SENSITIVITY - this is living in the present moment and allowing yourself to just **be. Listening** to your inner, instead of just hearing. **Seeing** the big picture, instead of just looking. **Perceiving feelings** from soul to soul like a radar system. This way, you really understand and know what is happening and the words "I don't know" will never enter your head. We perceive far more from what we do not say than what is actually said in words.

All behaviour that goes against these guidelines, keeps the planet in the sad state that it is in.

Volcanoes erupting, earthquakes, floods, droughts, thunderstorms etc, are caused by our behaviour towards ourselves and nature and our fellow man. Mother Earth is saying, *"I've had enough!"*

LOVE KNOWS NO BOUNDARIES.

LOVE YOURSELF AND THE PLANET WILL BE HEALED.

"Life Is An Adventure. See The Joy In Every Experience."

CHAPTER 4

QUALITIES WE COME TO LEARN

Our purpose in life is to grow spiritually and raise our level of consciousness to become **one** with all things.

Many people say that they do not know what their purpose is.

It does not matter what profession or field of work you do, we all come to learn certain qualities.

We are evolving souls and our need is to keep growing. We are unhappy when we are stagnating or procrastinating.

Our guidance know what our purpose is and they lead us into situations where we can best learn the qualities that we have come to learn, but if we don't - we just keep being put into similar situations again and again until we do learn it.

My big learning experience was when our car landed upside down across the road after skidding on a gravel road into an embankment. I was always catering to people and not standing up for myself. This was shown to me loud and clear that I needed to change those concepts. This growth completely overshadowed the inconvenience of not having a car for two months.
When we **learn** from a very hurtful experience, it takes all the hurt away because we know we have grown from it and can then help others with that knowledge. Then we will be better equipped for our next experience.

Being **INVOLVED** to master something makes us feel **SUCCESSFUL** and **FULFILLED** and these three are the ingredients for inner peace.

Here is a list of eighteen qualities for you to check which ones you have come to empower into your consciousness and see which ones you have already mastered.

1.	Balance	10.	Flexibility
2.	Beingness	11.	Freedom
3.	Compassion	12.	Fulfilment.
4.	Consideration	13.	Giving
5.	Creativity	14.	Humility
6.	Detached	15.	Loyalty
7.	Determination	16.	One with all
8.	Discernment	17.	Patience.
9.	Enjoyment	18	Responsibility

"To See What Is Right And Not To Do It, Is Want Of Courage" -Confucius

The following is an understanding for each quality:-

1. BALANCE

While you are here on this planet with a physical body you are simply borrowing all these material things to learn from, not be possessed by them. Always make goals for your needs and wants to be up-graded but for the balance, you must write down also what you want to **learn** from each of your goals. This is the spiritual and physical balance you need.
The money will just come if you are learning from your material things.

Love and greed is the other balance you need - the good and the bad, the right and the wrong. Use all your so called "bad" experiences from which to gain wisdom so you can use them to show or help others that it is no big deal when you learn and move on.

2. BEINGNESS

It is using all your inner power to be yourself and in your own energy, no matter what negativity is around you. It is your childlike self, living in your feelings and letting others do the same. When you are in control of your own power, you are not wanting to control others. You are simply being yourself and that beingness is the power you seek and it is inside you, not outside you. It is that "still inside" feeling of knowing who you are, where you came from, what you are doing here, and where you are going.

If you are without direction and do not know what you want, other people will tell you, then you are wasting your time. If you are just being, there is no need to prove anything to anyone.

The sermon on the mount by Jesus *(Matthew Chapter. 5 Verses. 3 - 11)* proclaims blessed attitudes and it's true meaning is hidden by naming them "Beatitudes" These are simply **attitudes** of **beingness** for us to just **BE**. Not to just live that beingness in a meditation. Take that feeling into every day life to just be your childlike self.

3. COMPASSION

If you have come to learn compassion, you could be pretty good at **judging** because that is it's opposite.

The surest way to eliminate judging is as soon as you criticize something in someone, just say to yourself - "How do **I** do that?" If you read in Chakra 7, "Our eyes only see what we need to see and grow from, so what we see in others we have in ourselves". If it aggravates you, you have that concept or attitude quite badly. If you notice it and it does not "jar" you, you have got over it.

Continued ......

"You Will Never Have Any More Time Than You Have Today."

The saying - "It takes one to know one", is quite applicable here. You are usually not doing it in the same way as the other person but still you are doing it, and that is what you can change. The other person then will not annoy you.

The compassion you seek is mostly for yourself, so when you learn to show it to yourself, you will then show it to others and more loving relationships towards others flow from you. It is allowing yourself to be yourself and allowing others to be themselves.

4. CONSIDERATION

"Whatever ye would that men should do to you, do ye even so to them." This is the golden rule - in other words - I will consider you and I would like you to consider me.
Think back to your childhood, most parents haven't shown us consideration. They do not treat us as a soul. We are a soul in a physical body and just because that body is little, they treat us as though we do not know anything. They do everything for us and stop us from growing.

They say, do things their way, instead of letting us use our own creativity. They treat us like babies and do not explain why they tell us to do things - just do it! We need to understand, because up until the age of seven years we are only feelings. This lack of consideration makes us rebel by getting sick so we worry our parents, but of course it affects us in the long run. Also at that time we converse freely with our guidance and then we are belittled for talking to ourselves and that cuts us off from our inner knowings and our potential.

Be considerate to yourself and put yourself first always, then you will do the same for others.

5. CREATIVITY

Using your inner resources to bring about new ideas so you progress (a soul needs to keep evolving) to better ways to do things. Blockages, or so called failures, bring about your creative talents to solve problems to find different avenues of learning. There is always a solution, if only you look inside yourself for your answers and insights. Being creative and using your imagination stops any hints of boredom and keeps you out of a rut.

6. DETACHED

Life would be so relaxed if we all practised staying detached. When someone tells you their troubles, what usually happens is they go off feeling better because they have off-loaded them onto you and you feel so bad and sorry for that person. The idea is just to listen, you may suggest something that has worked for you, but stay detached with a live and let live attitude and keep minding your own business.

You need strong boundaries for this quality's lesson.

Follow the example of your Guidance. They will never tell you what to do. They love you too much to interfere with your free will.

It is only earth bound souls who will tell you what to do. It is your negativity that allows this to happen.

Respect people for where they are at and accept them when they challenge your patience. Notice their good qualities and just get on with doing your purpose in life. Nobody needs to be saved.

7. DETERMINATION

Determination is not stubborn or pig-headedness. It is being directed to follow through with your plan to be successful.

It is staying on your pivot point or in your own energy and keeping strong boundaries for what you want and need and going for it.

Being single eyed to achieve for yourself is required here. It is putting yourself first with an unwavering mind.

8. DISCERNMENT

So that you can be confident in everything you do, you need to discern all the **facts** before you do anything. You don't build your house without a plan. Firstly, you think of a plan, then you visualize the plan, then you discern the vision and that gives you all the facts before you go and build it with confidence.

Your discernment could come from an inner knowing or a vision or an intuitive thought or a feeling.

Discern your first impression - that is what to follow always and understand that your second and third thoughts that come in to your head is that intellect that wants to talk you out of doing what is best for you.

Continued ......

"Fortunate People Are Those Who Believe They Are."

Continued ......

When you have that discernment of knowing exactly what it is you want and how to get it, you go for it and you don't let others put you off with their likes and dislikes.

Use your sensitivity or your radar system to get a feeling for everything you do. That **feeling** or first impression is what you need to discern so you get your timing right and the reasons why you are doing it.

Discernment is understanding and to perceive clearly and that is what you need to do about yourself. When you understand yourself and why you do the things you do, you may want to change and grow from that learning. When you have discernment, you have enthusiasm and power.

9. ENJOYMENT

When you keep things light and happy, you are able to learn more and take it into your feelings. Then when you take things in, you can give them out and that is where your enjoyment comes.

Being involved is also instrumental in giving enjoyment.

You need to be solid in your inner knowing of who you are and what you are doing, so you can be with all different personalities and not be put off by them. Your positivity creates enjoyment to you and to others.

10. FLEXIBILITY

This quality brings growth. If you are rigid and in a rut, keeping on the same track, never daring to leave your comfort zone, you are only existing and deadly boring. A new road is exciting and not to be feared.

Nothing happens to you that you cannot handle. Experience new things and new places. Change from being habitually predictable. Plan your day to only 70% so you allow for any unforeseen experience to crop up.

Be prepared to down tools and move when spirit gives you an insight or a hunch to change direction. Go for it! Live in the present moment and follow your feelings. If you have a stiff neck, it is a sure sign you are inflexible. Tradition and being set in your ways blocks growth.

"When You Trust Yourself, There Is Nothing To Worry About."

11. FREEDOM

When you have this quality, you are being responsible for your life. Be in control of yourself to know that Mother Earth supports you and the universe provides for you. Guilt from the past, worry for the future and a fear of lacking are all limitations that stop your freedom. Unlimit your limitless self. Through listening to your inner feelings, you obtain understanding of why you let yourself hang on to those limitations and fears. Letting go of them is your freedom. When you are free you can experience the unknown without engaging in fear. Learn more and enjoy being free to live in the present moment. Dare to be defenceless and fearless. See and hear what is here, instead of what should be, was, or will be. Say what you feel instead of what you think you should. Feel what you feel instead of what you ought. Ask for what you want, instead of waiting for permission. Take risks on your own behalf instead of choosing to be secure and not rock the boat. Just be yourself.

12. FULFILLMENT

This is the feeling you have when you have successfully achieved a job well done. It is being able to plan, then visualise that plan, discern the picture and organize what to do, when to do it, where to do it and why you are doing it and to keep the vision of the finished opportunity in mind so that your enthusiasm is always there to follow it through to the finish.

Making short-term and long-term goals is essential for this learning experience as much as doing it for yourself is important.

13. GIVING

This is our most natural quality as it gives us great pleasure when we give and see the joy of the other person receiving it. But we need to have it in balance. Learn to receive as well as give. Think of a jug of water. If we pour some out, we have space to add more. If you breathe out and keep breathing out, you have to take a breath in. So there must be give and take in balance.

The world is all LOVE and GREED and we know which way the scales have been tipped - Now we are wanting to go too much the other way and give too much to make up for it. We do not want do-gooders, caterers or savers.

It is best not to do more than 50% for people because you take away their opportunity to learn and grow. If you have to do 100% for someone make sure you are learning something for yourself from this opportunity.

When you do give -- give without hooks or without expecting in return and that is when it feels good.

Continued ......

"Balancing Your Giving And Receiving Makes For Healthy Living."

Sometimes if there has not been an equal energy exchange we sense something is wrong.

When we give of our knowledge, we are learning for ourselves as we teach what we need to learn. This knowledge gets locked into our feelings as we give it to others and that is how it becomes wisdom and that is what we take with us when we leave.

14. HUMILITY

It is the opposite to Glory. It doesn't mean to lower yourself. It means to just **be yourself** without being a know all or greater than anyone else. Know yourself and feel comfortable with others, work and grow with them. Treat others as your equal. We all have good points. Take note of everything positive in people as they reflect yourself..

Feelings of humility are when you know who you are, what you are doing here and where you are going and knowing the big picture.

You are humble when you are being of service. (Do not be a servant.)

15. LOYALTY

This means to put yourself first. We have come here to be loyal to ourselves first, not to any family or any organization. No one can breathe for you, no one can eat for you and no one can raise your level of consciousness and only your loyalty to yourself can accomplish this.

Use your intuition to find what is the big picture that spirit has for you and be loyal to it - No "Avoid-Dancing!" When you are loyal to yourself, you will travel first class and achieve your goals with ease.

16. ONE WITH ALL

It is having no separation from yourself (your own true feelings) or from minerals, plants, animals or from people, or God, or the Universe.

When you are being your own true love and respecting yourself and others where they are, you can stay relaxed and there is no outside pressure. That is when you are one with all. You are no greater or lesser than anyone. Competition is the opposite to being one with all. The only competition you need, is a little to stimulate you into enthusiasm to become involved.

Working with others in teamwork is a test for this quality.

*"A Dogma Is **NOT** Spiritual. It Is Like A Police Officer Telling You Where You Have To Drive."*

17. PATIENCE

Patience with yourself first is essential and your need to be strong within yourself to not let other people's energy affect you.

It is the power within, to be able to take the blame and not be blaming others when it is most probably caused by you anyway.

It is forgiving and forgetting if you have let yourself be hurt.

It is being yourself and seeing where others are at and letting them be that way and not let it upset or worry you. If you can see something in a person that annoys you, you know you have it in you in some form. They are doing you a favour for showing it to you really.

When you accept yourself you will accept others. That is the patience that you are striving for.

People grow in their own timing and we sometimes would like to put a bomb under them. This is no use, until the person understands for themselves what it is they need to change. Then they may see the light and do something about it.

18. RESPONSIBILITY

Your life is your business and you have to take responsibility for it. You are the only one who is in charge of your life. What happens to you in any situation is nobody else's fault but yours. You cannot blame anyone else. You let it happen to you.

You can make things happen if you so desire -

"If it's to be - it's up to me."

Find out what you like doing best in the world and that is your profession for this lifetime. If you are earning your living from what you love doing, that is when you will be happy.

If you **have to** do something you don't enjoy it is because that is obligation, but when there is responsibility you feel you **want to** do it.

It is your responsiblity to enjoy yourself this lifetime. You did not come to suffer -- The Spiritual way is simple and loving.

"If You Wake Up And Find You Are A Success,
You Haven't Been Asleep!"

CHAPTER 5

CONCEPTS THAT WILL KEEP YOU EARTH BOUND OR IN LIMBO

The following list has concepts that we may have that are limiting us and holding us back from being ourselves and using our full potential. When we shed these concepts, we can enjoy our life.

If we do not look at ourselves and own up to doing these concepts we are not being honest with ourselves.

One way to find out if you have any of them, is to listen to yourself when you describe someone else. If you can see it in others you have it in you in varying degrees - It may be only slightly but you grow spiritually by recognizing it and letting it go.

If you do not discard these concepts this lifetime, when you snap your silver cord and pass over or make your transition, you will float on out to your level of consciousness and hang around either as an earthbound soul near earth or be in limbo, just waiting around doing nothing until you reincarnate again. Why not get on with it this lifetime while you have the chance. It is your responsibility to yourself.

The main reasons for becoming an earthbound soul is that you were either possessive, you had strong likes or dislikes, you were into control or you just did not understand or even query what your life was all about.

Do you see now how essential it is for you to change your ways and not be caught up in these negative earthly energies.

Now do you know where hell is? It is hell on earth keeping these concepts! Being earth bound or being in limbo is the hell that we are told about. You **can** call it hell because the soul is not evolving when it is locked into these set ways of thinking. To be happy, a soul needs to be involved in learning, growing, changing, evolving and enjoying itself.

Be sincere and have the concern for yourself to rid yourself of these debilitating concepts and be the love that you are -- your true essence.

"A Wish Bone Has Never Taken The Place Of A Backbone."

THESE CONCEPTS WILL KEEP YOU EITHER EARTHBOUND OR IN LIMBO

CHAKRA No 1 will be affected by the following concepts:-

EARTHBOUND CONCEPTS	LIMBO CONCEPTS
Blocked	Impatience
Dissatisfaction	Insecure
Inadequate	Intolerant
No communication	No confidence
Not in charge of self	No discernment
Not knowing what to do next	No inner authority
Unworthiness	No memory
	No self-acceptance
	Not getting facts
	Too old
	Unbalanced
	Unloved
	Vanity

CHAKRA No 2 will be affected by the following concepts:-

Not going after wants	Lack of abundance
No goals	(scarcity)
Thieving	

CHAKRA No 3 will be affected by the following concepts:-

Competition
Conceited
Defiant
Not going after needs
Not trusting
Not wanting to do what I need
Sex offences (over sexed)

CHAKRA No 4 will be affected by the following concepts:-

Aggravation (anger)	Alone
Bitterness	Always feel a failure
Deception	Anti Spiritual teaching
Deviant	Apprehensive
Disharmony	Bewilderment
Doubting	Brash
Fearful	Corrupt
Fighting	Coveting
Frustration	Dependency
Guilt	Emotional
Hatred	Enjoy your own tragedies
Have to win	Envy

Continued ......

Continued ......

CHAKRA No 4

Indecision	Expecting
Jealousy	Expecting Reward
Lack of direction	Greedy
Lack of purpose	Hermit - recluse
Lack of sensitivity	Lack of enjoyment
No feelings	Lack of respect
Not good enough	Neglect
Not sincere	Never feel successful
Not understanding	Not changing
Over eating (gluttonous)	Over sleeping
Pressure	Rigid-inflexible
Resentment	Sadness
Separation	Selfish
Scatty	Stubborn
Spite	Unfulfilled
Stopping growth	Unjust
Suffering	Waiting for approval
Trickery	Worry
Violence	
Yearning	

CHAKRA No 5 will be affected by the following concepts:-

Catering
Lack of enthusiasm
Outside devotion

CHAKRA No 6 will be affected by the following concepts:-

Abrasive	Begrudging
Ambiguity	Chauvinist
Attack	Fault finding
Blaming	Indifference
Bullying	Judgment
Caustic	Unco-operative
Distractions	
Hostile	
Lack of compassion	
Minding other people's business	
Not believing	
Petty	
Small minded	
Vicious	

CHAKRA No 7 will be affected by the following concepts:-

Aggressive
Beligerant
Bigotry
Control
Deprivation
Destructive - Vandalism
Fighting other people's battles
Fragmentation
Glory
Hopelessness
Lack of judgement for doing
Laziness
Not businesslike
Not comprehending
  & putting it into practise
Not creative
Not doing one step at a time
Not organized
Not resourceful
Possessiveness
Pride
Punishment
Religious
 (churchianity not Christianity)
Resistance
Revenge
Righteous

Analysing & dissecting
Cannot be told (know all)
Cannot see the future
Cautious
Conform
Fixed picture
Greater than lesser than
Have to
Have to prove things
Hesitant
Lack of action
Lack of consideration
No boundaries
No distinction between
  Personal, Business & Social
No follow through
Not compact
Not controlling self
Not flowing
Not seeing the big picture
Not sharing (holding back)
Not using full potential
Others first
Poor little me (sorry for self)
Prestigious
Procrastination
Raciness
Saying "I can't"
Self-centred
Sensationalist
Should be beautiful
Should be good
Should be true
Slowness
Submissive (subserviant)
Timing
Tradition
Uncommitted
What will people think

CHAPTER 6

POSITIVE CONCEPTS OF THE TEETH

CHAKRA 7 - OUTFLOW - UPPER TEETH

OVERALL CONCEPT -   What the plan will be like when finished.
Seeing the big picture of the plan.

UPPER LEFT - SPIRITUAL

1st. INCISOR   Find out all ideas.
2nd. INCISOR   What will it feel like?
      CANINE   (Cuspid/Eye tooth) Believe in the plan.
1st. BICUSPID   (Premolar) Discernment of the plan ensures success.
2nd. BICUSPID   (Premolar) Evaluate the situation before planning.
1st. MOLAR   When you know, plan for involvement.
2nd. MOLAR   Plan is organized, so proceed.
3rd. MOLAR   (Wisdom) Understand your inner feelings before creating.

UPPER LEFT

INCISOR   BICUSPID   MOLAR

CANINE

UPPER RIGHT - PHYSICAL

1st. INCISOR   Question every needed aspect.
2nd. INCISOR   Look at every aspect.
      CANINE   (Cuspid/Eye tooth) Imagine the end result.
1st. BICUSPID   (Premolar) Work out the entire plan.
2nd. BICUSPID   (Premolar) Be thorough when organizing every detail.
1st. MOLAR   Bring about what is needed.
2nd. MOLAR   Your thoughts need to create involvement.
3rd. MOLAR   (Wisdom) Use all the facts for your achievement.

UPPER RIGHT

MOLAR   BICUSPID   INCISOR

CANINE

CHAKRA 1 - INFLOW - LOWER TEETH

OVERALL CONCEPT - Planning for new experiences.

LOWER LEFT - SPIRITUAL

1st. INCISOR How is it meant to be?
2nd. INCISOR Will it be able or efficiently function?
CANINE (Cuspid/Eye tooth) Sense the way it works.
1st. BICUSPID (Premolar) Being prepared for oncoming happenings.
2nd. BICUSPID (Premolar) Do things when you have organized.
1st. MOLAR Always be careful to analyze.
2nd. MOLAR Chew over things when choosing procedures.
3rd. MOLAR (Wisdom) Being thorough comes from using feelings.

CANINE

INCISOR BICUSPID MOLAR

LOWER LEFT

LOWER RIGHT - PHYSICAL

1st. INCISOR You need all reasons available understood.
2nd. INCISOR Find new ways to experiment when seeking involvement.
CANINE (Cuspid/Eye tooth) For order, you must organize.
1st. BICUSPID (Premolar) See all the information that is necessary.
2nd. BICUSPID (Premolar) Understand every detail so that it is practical.
1st. MOLAR Make sure to trust the sensitivity needed regularly.
2nd. MOLAR Be fearless, so be honest and forceful.
3rd. MOLAR (Wisdom) Believe success can be achieved with determination.

CANINE

MOLAR BICUSPID INCISOR

LOWER RIGHT

ORGANS ASSOCIATED WITH THE 7 CHAKRAS

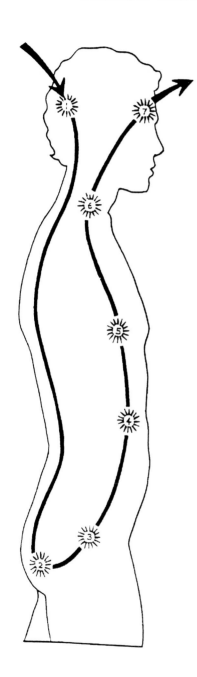

1. **PINEAL** - Self Acceptance
   Nose
   Ears
   Lower Teeth
   Sublingual Glands
   Hypothalmus
   Thalamus
   Back of Brain

2. **COCCYX** - Wants
   Adrenals
   Kidneys
   Bladder
   Appendix
   Large Intestine

3. **REPRODUCTIVE AREA** - Needs
   Uterus - Prostate
   Ovaries - Scrotum or Testes
   Vagina - Penis
   Ovum - Sperm (Semen)

4. **SOLAR PLEXUS** - Identity
   Pancreas
   Spleen
   Stomach
   Liver
   Gall Bladder
   Small Intestine

5. **HEART** - Devotion to Self
   Thymus
   Heart
   Circulatory System
   Breasts
   Lungs
   Diaphragm
   Lymphatic System
   Immune System

6. **THYROID** - Relating
   Thyroid
   Parathyroids
   Tonsils
   Throat
   Larynx
   Pharynx
   Parotid Glands
   Submaxillary Glands

7. **PITUITARY** - Outflow
   Eyes
   Vocal Cords
   Mouth
   Front of Brain
   Third Eye
   Upper Teeth

46

CHAPTER 7

CHAKRAS - YOUR ENERGY CENTRES

All around you, you have an aura. You can **feel** that energy field when you rub your hands together a little, then bring them apart and the sensation you feel in between your hands is the energy of your aura, your soul.

You can also **see** that aura field all around your body and it changes colour with the way you are feeling. When you are learning and enjoying yourself, it is wide and colourful. If you are sick or depressed it is close, thin and grey. Who wants to be near a person whose aura is like the latter?

The following chapters on each of the seven chakras will help you to **know** and **understand** your aura or soul part as well. How it needs to be thinking to keep each area of the body in good working order.

The soul part of you is what governs your body and the seven main chakras controlling the different areas of your body. So the way you are thinking is the reason for your body to let you know that your thought patterns are needing to be looked into.

The chakras are where energy is distributed throughout the body and they are there to control the body. So how you are thinking in your soul is the power that is available to each cell in your body.

When your thinking is positive, the right amount of energy is kept flowing through to keep the cells healthy.

Each chakra needs to be having the positivity of the right thoughts of each one, as each one is for a different learning experience. Therefore, you must understand the positive way your thoughts are to be channelled.

Your time on earth here is spent experiencing emotions of fear, greed, murder, judgment and aloneness, which are all so negative that they have to be controlled, because your reactions to them are the thoughts that eat into your cells and give you your ailments.

Be responsible for yourself and your planet. Get back to your own true feelings of being one with all and those positive thoughts of your beingness will give power to your chakras to heal your body and keep your cells alive and rejuvenated.

"We Are What We Are Because Of Our Thinking."

The different learning experiences are covered in each chakra chapter but the simple over view of your seven chakras is:- When you are here with a body you are in the physical or material world, not the spiritual as you are without a body. The Coccyx and Reproductive chakras are concerned with what you want and need to have while here. When you realize that you are a spiritual being in your physical body, you know there is more to life than earthly things, and you have only come to borrow these and use them to learn from. That is when you begin to spiral upwards with your state of consciousness.

The first thing with your inflow chakra is to be **patient** and **accept yourself** and know that you have the power to go after what you want and need. Then you are being **loyal to yourself** and obtaining things without **competition**.

The next step is that of understanding in the solar plexus of just, who you are. The maturity that comes from this understanding leads you to be **positive** to start learning and growing from everything you do. That leads you to loving yourself in your heart chakra. Being **devoted to yourself** by doing for you and doing it your way.

When you have all those positive feelings for yourself, you can relate to others with **compassion** and without judging them for your thyroid chakra, for the simple reason, you are being that way towards yourself now.

By having all that understanding of yourself and others you can outflow in a **humble** way, or with **humility**. Just being and giving out your skills and being of service and speaking from your true feelings. Now there is your whole life and how to live it and know what having purpose can accomplish.

GUIDELINES FOR YOUR THINKING

- **I am a soul with a physical body.**
  Know who I am.
- **Put myself first.**
  Love myself.
- **Learn and grow from everything I do.**
  Be involved and do for myself.
- **Everything happens for a purpose.**
  Stumbling blocks are just stepping stones.
- **Change your concepts that affect your body.**
  Know that you are in charge of your destiny.
- **Be of service, not a servant.**
  Give 50% and take 50%.

"See Beyond The Obvious."

COLOURS FOR THE CHAKRAS

Your chakras respond to colours, whether you just tell yourself you are putting colours through them or visualizing the colours going into them or wearing the colours that will stimulate your chakra. The effect can be quite pronounced. Because colours have energy and they stimulate the chakra to a certain extent, it is good to know the energy they give off.

It helps the chakra to have a certain colour vibration to stimulate it into it's kind of action.

1   PINEAL (INFLOW) - RED

This chakra will benefit and be stimulated into action by red which is vibrant and gives forth **ACTION** and **VITALITY**.

2   COCCYX - ORANGE

The colour orange gives forth strong feelings of **UNDERSTANDING** and **COURAGE** which can help your coccyx to obtain it's wants.

3   REPRODUCTIVE - YELLOW

The yellow colour vibrates **ENERGY** and **UNIVERSAL LOVE** needed to go after what you need.

4   SOLAR PLEXUS - GREEN

The colour green is for **REALITY** and **GROWTH** for knowing who you are in your solar plexus.

5   HEART - BLUE

The colour blue gives off the feeling of **BELONGING** and **HEALING** for your heart chakra to love self and give motivation.

6   THYROID - PURPLE

The colour purple has a **ONE WITH ALL** and **LOYALTY** feeling to give to your relating chakra to stimulate harmony.

7   PITUARY (OUTFLOW) - WHITE

The colour white vibrates **BEINGNESS** and **PEACE** in giving love.

"A Smile Is A Curve That Straightens Out A Lot Of Things."

WHITE has no hue due to the **REFLECTION** of all or almost all incident light. It consists of all the colours of the spectrum. When the sun hits other colours, it is reflected on to you and you can gain it's energy.

BLACK has no hue, due to the **ABSORPTION** of all, or nearly all, incident light and will soak up all the light so that you are unable to have that light shine on to you. The energy is blocked by black and you gain nothing. Black will block the way energy penetrates.

If you have a dislike for a colour, meditate on it to find the reason. Once you understand the cause, you will come back to liking it.

There is disagreement on what colour stimulates each chakra. You all have your answers and solutions inside you to varify what you think.

I have followed the rainbow spectrum order in this book. In my previous book, I simply followed what I had been taught, but I found that the green comes before the blue in the spectrum. The solar plexus really needs green because that is where we begin our growth and the heart needs blue for healing, love and belonging.

HEALING IS SIMPLE

A woman came to see me one day and she told me she had a sore throat and she related the experience she had had the night before. I then explained to her that her throat was only sore because of her thoughts and she understood that she needed to change them to a live and let live attitude. We went on discussing other matters and in little over an hour she exclaimed - "My sore throat has gone". Now that is how simple healing really is. Understand what your chakra needs and your body will be free of pain.

The mind is the powerful healer that will cure anything if you want it to.

"A Wise Man Will Make More Opportunities Than He Finds."
- Francis Bacon

CHAPTER 8

CHAKRA No 1

PINEAL - INFLOW - SELF ACCEPTANCE

THE CONCEPT TO KEEP IT HEALTHY IS "PATIENCE"

"IMPATIENCE" WILL CAUSE TROUBLE IN: NOSE, EARS, LOWER TEETH, SALIVARY GLAND.(SUBLINGUAL), HYPOTHALAMUS, THALAMUS and BACK OF BRAIN.

We are spiritual beings with a physical body. Our bodies are made up of all parts of planet earth. The spiritual part we call our soul is intelligent energy -- Your entire feelings from experiences from lifetime after lifetime. This energy of your soul or life force or your inner being keeps the cells of your body alive and it flows in through your pineal gland, the crown chakra.

People who deny this spiritual energy coming to them, by thinking that their No 1 chakra is the Base chakra, accept from planet earth the base energies of planet earth such as the vibrations of greed, lust, envy and religious dominance etc.

If they would only accept the crown chakra as their energy inflow point, their spiritual sensitivity (Feelings) would be heightened and they would **not** be dependant on gurus for their direction, which has given them an earthly **intellectual** spiritual outlook. They are not using **their own** insights for their own full potential.

You all have inner Guidance, Guardian Angels, Spiritual Helpers or Master Souls, whatever you like to call them. They are your own personal teachers to guide you from the human level up to the spiritual level where they are. They can guide you because they have the big overview of your life. They will never tell you what to do, they love and respect you too much to interfere with your free will.

Therefore, take a big deep "dolphin-like" breath which is inspiration and you will receive inspiration from within you.

Total acceptance of yourself is wanted for this chakra for you to totally accept the world around you. You can then be relaxed and patient so you can receive all your insights from within you for your own specific purpose that you are here to experience and learn from and enjoy.

"If Everyone Approves Of What You Are Doing, I Urge You To Reconsider What You Are Doing." Saint Germain

To help you find a little of your purpose, I have listed eighteen qualities in Chapter 4 that you could choose your specific ones for you to focus on and learn.

When you are patient with yourself and others, you are relaxed and you will receive the insights that you need to have you in the right place at the right time.

Tolerance of self and others allows you to accept more inflow and learn to take in more. Intolerant people go deaf.

Being satisfied, often comes from learning new things and putting self first and following through on your first impression to completion.

Listen for your inspirations and inner knowings. Trust your communication from within. These new ideas are for you to move on. These are your plans for the future. See that plan working and when to take action on it and work out what you need when you decide to do it.

Think of a time when you did follow your first impression. Did it give you a feeling of satisfaction and fulfilment? Now, think of a time when you procrastinated and missed out. What a different feeling!

With the former, you had all the **facts** so you were confident and you did not listen to the second or third thoughts that came into your head. (Your intellect with the "what ifs?" etc.) or you were not put off by other people's ideas.
When you receive your first impression, use the five P's --

"**P**rior **P**reparation **P**revents **P**oor **P**erformance"

and that means finding out the "what", "when" "where" and "why" of it and getting on with it.

FEAR is when you have not used your inflow to establish the facts.

"**F**antasy **E**xpectations **A**ppearing **R**eal"

DOUBT is "**D**riving **O**urselves **U**nconscious **B**y **T**hinking"

which is what happens when you listen to those second or third thoughts that come to you.

For every step, make sure you have a solution. Follow your **feelings** which are creative and powerful and use your **intellect** for finding the facts only. Not the fantasies and assumptions. Your feelings must be in control. Your intellect has to be kept in check and not cause you to procrastinate.

"Creativity Is Putting Inspiration Into Action."

Discover what methods you use to fragment yourself to keep you from doing what is best for you or what you came to do. It could be by not using the inspirations that come from your dreams. Saying they are silly or scary. Dreams are a daily source of inspiration that you need to interpret from their symbols. *See Dreams Chapter.*

Do you ever keep singing the same song over and over like a cracked record? My husband used to say "How about changing that record!" Then I would take note of the words of the song and I would realize that there was a message or an insight for me to think about. Once I understand the message, the compulsion to sing it ceases.

If you are not relaxed enough to let your Guidance through, they may talk through other people to tell you what you need to hear.

You may see things that remind you of something because they cannot give you insights when you are racing around and disorganized.

Sometimes, they talk through me to others, but it is for my understanding as well.

Another sure way I obtain my insights is from an ailment in my body.

Your body communicates to you that you have an ailment, then you need honest communication with yourself to find out what you are doing to cause that ailment.

If you have any problems with your car, it will point out what is wrong with your direction. *See Car Chapter.*

Can you see that there are many ways you can receive insights that help to keep this chakra in order?

There are learning experiences everywhere for your spiritual growth to keep the energy flowing through your chakras and keep your body free from pain. Your Guides are there to help you understand those experiences.

Your soul's plan is to grow spiritually so it is a must for your growth that you make time for yourself each day to be at one with yourself and reflect on what you have learned about yourself and whether you need to do things differently next time.

To be out in the fresh air, near water or near trees on your own, to just feel one with nature will encourage more insights.

"Life Is Like Climbing A Tree. The Higher You Climb,
The More You Can See."

Have you noticed how a baby breathes when asleep? The stomach moves, not the chest. Remember to use your diaphragm and breathe that way too. Breathe deeply. If you have trouble breathing, you are not enjoying life.

With the will to live you need self-esteem, self respect, self acceptance and the inner authority to put yourself first. Knowing that you have as much right as anyone else on this planet. This shows you that you need that inner authority to stand up for yourself, to make boundaries for yourself. Have the ability to tell people how far they can go with you and what you want. It is actually commanding respect for yourself. When you respect yourself, you naturally have respect for others.

If you have created authority figures, recognize them and let go and have more patience with yourself. You do not need that sort of limitation. Be yourself always in all situations.

If you have let yourself get down and depressed and have lost your will to live, your Guidance can not lift you out of that emotional state, but if you take a step out of that rut, they can and will help you, just ask. They will give you all the backing you need when you begin to help yourself.

Try going through your cupboards and throw out your old material possessions that you do not need. You will find fresh energy coming in to replace the old, in material form or insights.

"People's Minds Are Like Parachutes. To Function Properly
They Must First Be Open."

AILMENTS	YOUR ATTITUDES THAT STOP YOUR ENERGY FLOW THROUGH YOUR PINEAL AREA
AGORAPHOBIA (Dread of open spaces)	You have had an experience in the past which you have not understood. The **power** you need is **discernment** of the situation which will remove the fear. You can then be in charge of your emotions. Remember, everything happens for a purpose from which to learn.
BAD BREATH	Worrying instead of planning what to do first. You have gone sour on your plans and you are reacting to not having done them.
BLACKING OUT (FAINTING)	• Not wanting to face up to what you need to learn. • No plans because you are getting old. • All your plans are not acceptable now any more.
COLD SORES (Herpes simplex virus)	I do not want to take in that news.
CONCUSSION	Needing more inflow (new insights) You do not want to know what you need to hear.
DANDRUFF	A clogging up of your self-acceptance. Impatience with the way others do things. It is not the same way as I want them done.
DIZZINESS (Vertigo)	Not taking time for yourself. (Personal time) Going round in circles and not being organized for the straight path. Need more inflow of insights for what to do next. Make solid direction for self.
EARS	**Intolerance**. You do not want to listen to others or nobody is listening to you.
EARS BLOCKED	Impatience and intolerance with yourself at not knowing how you will be when you arrive at your destination.
EARS HOT	Getting hot or annoyed or being intolerant of someone's behavior.
EAR INFECTION	Stagnating, impatience and not tolerating new information.

EAR - SKIN PEELING	Not wanting to listen to a new concept that is a better way to do something.
EAR - WAX IN	Not wanting to listen to new things.
EPILEPSY	Not accepting the way you do things.
FALLING OVER	Lack of co-ordination. Not sure of self. Must have self-acceptance to feel secure within.
GANGRENE	Destroying yourself because you do not have any enthusiasm to love yourself.
GINGIVITIS	Putting off doing things. Stirred up emotions of incapability or fears.
GLANDULAR FEVER	Not accepting yourself and not wanting to be told. Your **pineal gland** is for taking in new things but you are just living in the past. Start living in the present and be open to new things. Your tiredness comes from outflowing and not taking in new insights. *(See Pineal Gland.)*
GOUT	When you are controlling others or being controlled, you are not accepting yourself either way, by allowing it to happen. When you **control** yourself and **accept yourself**, all your **worries** cease.
GUMS - BLEEDING	Pressurizing yourself because you are putting off doing things.
GUMS - RECEDING	Not doing things straight away because of lack of planning.
HAIR - BALDNESS ON CROWN	(Hair serves as an insulation and it grows in the skin which needs self-worth and feeling adequate) If it stops growing at the back of the head you are not insulating yourself with feelings of worthiness or of being adequate to accept yourself. (Some older men think they have reached a cycle that they are not capable of doing things the way they used to)
HAIR - DRY	Not being aware that you can achieve. Holding back because of your lack of beingness to direct your energy. Your inadequacy keeps you doing nothing because you do not know yourself.

HAIR - **FALLING OUT**	Hair is your insulation. You are not using your power of flexiblility to change your thinking. You must know that your own power is your insulation, not other people. You cannot rely on other people for your feelings of safety.
HAIR - GREYING Back of Head	(Hair is your insulation) (Pigment colour of hair is your perception of yourself) (Pineal Gland needs self-acceptance) If you are not accepting yourself, in some way you have changed your perception of yourself and the pigment drains out of your hair.
HAIR - GREYING **OVERNIGHT**	You let go of your power of beingness and enthusiasm, therefore (from shock) you have changed your **perception** of yourself and the **pigment** drained out of your hair.
HAIR - OILY	You put pressure on yourself with no patience by thinking you are inadequate from something you have not done in the past.
HAIR - **SPLIT ENDS**	You experience being vulnerable when your **insulation** of self-acceptance is not there.
HAY FEVER	Not **satisfied** with yourself.
HEADACHE Back of Head	Pressurizing yourself through impatience that you have not done enough.
HYPOTHALAMUS	Controls autonomic functions such as hunger and thirst satiety.It needs **freedom** so **restriction** goes against it's function.
MEMORY **(LACK OF)**	You do not think others are interested in what you know, so you think it is no use remembering what you know. The same with people. If you do not think they are interested in you, you forget their names or faces.
MENINGITIS	Stirred up emotions of not wanting to take in new insights. Being a know all is the reason.
MIGRAINE **Nervous** headache Back of head	Your **communication** to yourself that you are the one who needs to be accepted is not happening. Tell yourself you accept yourself no matter what has happened to you.
MULTIPLE **SCLEROSIS**	Lack of communication with others. When you accept yourself, you can communicate at any level without worrying what other people think of you.

NERVOUS BREAKDOWN	Not communicating to yourself that you have your own power of beingness, discernment and flexibility. You cannot blame anyone else but yourself for your problems because your power is within you. You need to "break through" to know this.
NOSE	Not willing to just be yourself.
NOSE - BLEEDING	Bursting a blood vessel! Not satisfied with self, so pushing yourself too hard to show that you are able to do things as well as others.
NOSE - BLOCKED	Not enjoying life.
NOSE - BROKEN	A rebellion to learning because of resentment.
NOSE (BULBOUS & RED)	Unworthy of living because everything you do goes against your feelings.
NOSE - PIMPLES INSIDE	Stagnating - holding on to the concept of not wanting to learn new things about yourself.
NOSE - RUNNING	Not satisfied with yourself if not learning.
PINEAL GLAND (Gateway to your POWER)	If you are not just **being**, you will not find your **direction**.
	If you are not **creative**, you will not **progress**.
	If you are not using your intuition for **discernment**, you will lack **enthusiasm**.
	If you are not being **flexible**, you will not **grow** in consciousness.
	Your **power** is made up of your beingness, creativity, discernment and flexibility and when you are living these concepts you will be accepting yourself.
SALIVA CAUSING PLAQUE	You do not plan how to get things done, you chew them over and over instead of getting them done. Prevalent in old people.
SALIVARY GLAND (Sublingual gland)	Not planning your insights to follow through.

SENILITY (Alzheimer's Disease) (Growing old at an early age)	• No one wants to communicate with you so why bother communicating with them. • You do not want to be in the situation that you are in of not knowing what to do with your life. • Not willing to stand up and change your life.
SINUS	Not enjoying life because you are not satisfied with the way you are not learning.
SNEEZING	Not accepting self in a way that you feel **cheated** because you are unable to see your good points.
STROKE	• Impatience with yourself for not improving a situation. • Impatience with yourself for not being able to perform like you want to. • Impatience with whatever has been done to you through injustice and blaming. Your pineal gland needs you to just **be**.With patience, your **beingness** shines through.
STUTTERING	You have had something done to you, to give you an inferiority complex. You need self-acceptance.
TEETH (Lower Only)	Planning for new experiences. *(For teeth detail see Chapter 6)* *(For top teeth, see Chakra 7)*
TEETH - ABSCESS	Stagnating by procrastinating with your plans.
TEETH - CUTTING	Thinking you will be unable to plan your purpose.
TEETH- DECAYING	Not planning new things which keeps you from changing.
TEETH - EXTRACTION	Losing your grip on life because you are not planning from your creative insights.
THALAMUS	Allows you to make **decisions. Criticism** of you will stop you making decisions.
TINNATUS	Intolerant to the point of screaming.
WHIPLASH	A jolt to tell you that you need more inflow (new insights)

WRINKLES   When you are not accepting yourself, and your life and think you have been dealt a raw deal. Feelings of worth do not fill out your skin and it is then you screw up your face with complaining and the expression stays there if you do not change this "victim consciousness".

YAWN   I want to learn more from what I am hearing or seeing.

CHAPTER 9

CHAKRA No 2 - COCCYX - WANTS

THE CONCEPT TO KEEP IT HEALTHY IS "LOYALTY TO SELF"

"DISLOYALTY TO SELF" WILL CAUSE TROUBLE IN: ADRENALS, KIDNEYS, BLADDER APPENDIX, and LARGE INTESTINE. (ASCENDING, TRANSVERSE & DESCENDING COLONS)

THE POSITIVE CONCEPTS FOR THE LARGE INTESTINE:

	(ASCENDING COLON	GENEROUS
SOCIAL	(TRANSVERSE COLON	OPENNESS
	(DESCENDING COLON	RELAXED

While you are here on planet earth in this body, you want to enjoy yourself. When you are loyal to yourself, you know you can have what you want so you can grow from what you have.

If you can think of it, you can have it.

Just make the decision and organize yourself to go after what you want and keep your vision of it always in mind. **You must know what you want** then no one else can tell you what you want and you are decisive and in control of your own life. The better you feel about yourself, the more you want for yourself. This gives you a feeling of affluence or abundance. When you realize that your material possessions are just on loan to you to learn from while you are here in the physical world, you will not be possessed by possessions.

You need a balance of Love and Greed in this physical world. When greed takes over, all you are thinking about is money and material possessions. The balance comes when you begin to understand that your possessions are for learning about yourself. How do you react when you lose a possession? How do you feel when someone gives you a present? Spiritual learning comes from being able to give and receive equally.

Never dwell on what you think you lack or what you think you can not have. Yearning will pull you down and depress you. Why do we always want what we think we do not have? Focus on what you have and all your good points.

People who steal things, know they are wanting something but it is their soul wanting **spiritual** understanding but they take it as wanting material things.

"Goals Are Dreaming With Deadlines."

You may have the desire for something but you must be **willing** to take **all** the required steps to attain that desire.

To keep the energy flowing through this chakra, you must have goals. Being active and involved in having goals and learning from them and gaining the feeling of achievement from them is being loyal to yourself. Having goals for your day, week, month, six months, one year and five years, is how to be successful and fulfilled. You feel secure and confident with goals for your direction.

If a goal does not come to fruition, check if you really need it. If you do not need it, make another in it's place. If you let go of your goals, you will cause diarrhoea, so always make new ones.

Be decisive with what you want and write down your goals. Your Guidance will then know you mean business. They will also know what to set up for you because they do their 50% for you and then you do your 50%.

Your life is divided into three areas:

PERSONAL   is the eight hours you need for yourself alone such as regrouping, (understanding self), sleeping, meditating and studying.

BUSINESS   is the eight hours you put into earning your living from giving out your time, knowledge and skills.

SOCIAL   is the eight hours you spend communicating with others. Each area needs to be balanced in it's spiritual and physical aspect.

The way I do it, is to take a sheet of paper, rule a line down the centre and two horizontal lines, first one, a third of the way down and the second one, two thirds down, so you have six equal squares as shown on the opposite page. Label the top three left squares as "Spiritual" and the top of the right squares as "Physical". The first two squares on top represent your Personal, the middle two represent your Business and the third two squares represent your Social.

Firstly, I write my personal spiritual goal in the top left square. Then in the physical side of the personal, I write how I want to manifest it in the physical.
For my business, I make my physical goal first of what I want and then in the spiritual left square -- what I want to learn from that goal. Then the money comes in. I **do not** at any stage make goals for money. As long as you want to learn from your physical goal your business will thrive.
For my social goals just whatever you need to enjoy it.

"Courage Is A Three Letter Word. Y.E.S!"

	SPIRITUAL	PHYSICAL
PERSONAL	Stop judging myself	Live and Let Live attitude with others
BUSINESS	Learn how to organize my time to keep business from overlapping in to my social time	Sell "X" amount of products each week
SOCIAL	Do not worry about what people think and be flexible	Learn to ski on my holiday

Put energy into your goals daily and simply put your thoughts of your wants to the universe. Do not dwell on them. When you have a written list, it takes the pressure from your memory.

When you know what you want always, you will not waste time because you are organized with your next opportunity.

When you are loyal to self, you are going first class through life.

You feel worthy and you value yourself because you know you deserve the best when learning for yourself.

Your **kidneys** are to do with **relationship wants**, especially the relationship you have with **yourself.** Take note of that first and then your relationship with others will improve.

When you are loyal to yourself first you can then help others.

Your large intestines are to do with your **outflow wants** and this represents your **SOCIAL** area of your life. To be loyal to yourself here is to be **generous, open** and **relaxed** when you are talking or working with people. When you cannot say what you feel to people, you will suffer from constipation.

"Courage Is The Finest Human Quality. It Guarantees All The Others."

AILMENTS	YOUR ATTITUDES THAT STOP YOUR ENERGY FLOW THROUGH YOUR COCCYX AREA.
ADRENALS	Loyalty to self is required for **action** - fears, doubt and no belief in self stops action so you do nothing.
ANUS - ITCHY	A recurring problem of not being able to outflow what you want to say or do.
APPENDICITIS	Stirred up emotions of wanting something but you do not think you can obtain it.
BED-WETTING (See Incontinence)	Not knowing how to get what you want.
BLADDER	Yearning.
BOWEL (Irritable Bowel Syndrome)	• Holding back, and keeping things to yourself rather than giving **generously** with what knowledge you have to give out.
	• Not being **open** in what you really feel.
	• Not being **relaxed** enough to give out your knowledge and share what you have.

CANDIDA - ALBICANS	It starts with you **doubting** yourself and this is the mouldy old concept you are not doing anything about. It affects:
	• Your adrenals - (Action) So when you doubt, you do nothing.
	• Your bladder - (Yearning for wants) You doubt that somehow you cannot obtain your wants.
Your {	• Your ascending colon (Generous)
Social {	• Your transverse colon (Openness)
Area {	• Your decending colon (Relaxed) *Your doubting stops all your outflow wants in your social life.*
	• Your bloating is the accumulation of any of these concepts.

Continued...

At this stage of our evolution, our bodies are changing as we are getting our DNA strands back together again as we grow in understanding. Candida and other dietary problems are directly related to this evolutionary process of the human body. They are there to show people that there are dietary changes that need to be implemented. People need to examine their diet and whether something is still beneficial to them or not. If it is no longer comfortable in their body, they are advised to stop using it permanently. Their body is saying that for the change it needs to make - this food is counter productive.

CONSTIPATION A bottling up of what you want to say, and not saying it.

CYSTITIS Burning inside because you cannot get what you want.

DEFAECATING It hurts you when you cannot say what you
(Pain when) want to say. Not able to outflow fluently.

DIARRHOEA Letting go of your goals when you decide you cannot have what you want.

DIVERTICULITIS Your emotions of being unsociable are stirred up
(Inflammation of a and you will not outflow your feelings.
diverticulum)

DIVERTICULUM Unsociable - so you do not want to outflow
(A pouch or sac in a your feelings *(see concepts of intestines
hollow organ, and bladder)*.
bladder or intestine)

DYSENTERY Cannot face what is going on. Digesting food is
understanding in your personal life for success.
(Solar plexus) but your food is just going straight through you without understanding because you have pressure from hating whatever you are seeing. So you want to let it out without taking it in before you outflow. You do not understand how you can have **empathy**, **knowing**, and **honesty** in your business life and be **generous**, **open** and **relaxed** while all this "whatever" is happening in your social life. **Understanding** is the concept of all **mucous membranes** and passing mucus because it was not used for understanding of what has happened gives you the gripes.

DYSENTERY - AMOEBIC An accumulation of the previous concepts.
(Giardia)

HAEMORRHOIDS You want to pass on your knowledge but you do
(Piles) not think it will be accepted.

HERNIA (Inguinal)	Angry with what is happening in your life and you do not know what to do about it.
INCONTINENCE	Guilty of not being loyal to yourself to go after your goals, because you do not know how to obtain your goals or wants. If old - Thinking that you are too old to go after new things.
INTESTINES - **LARGE** (Bowels)	**SOCIAL AREA - OUTFLOW WANTS**
ASCENDING **COLON**	**Generous.**Need to be generous to yourself first, then with others. Never leave yourself out.
TRANSVERSE **COLON**	**Openness**. Be open with yourself then it will be the same with others.
DECENDING **COLON**	**Relaxed**. When you are relaxed within yourself, you have no trouble to outflow and share in your social life with others.
KIDNEYS	**Relationship wants**. Firstly you need a good relationship with yourself, then you can have one with others.
KIDNEY - **CANCER**	You are giving up. You think you cannot do anything about the situation to have a good relationship with yourself or others.
KIDNEY - **FAILURE**	Being a "poor little me" about the situation. Saying you cannot have a good relationship with yourself or with someone else.
KIDNEY - **INFLAMMATION**	Stirred up emotions through relationship wants. Not making goals to have a smooth relationship with self or with others.
KIDNEY - **STONES**	Not having a good relationship with self or others and not doing anything about the situation. It gets solidified inside you.
KIDNEY - **TUMOUR**	You are not trusting yourself that you could be able to obtain your wants. You are being loyal to someone else instead of yourself. You leave yourself out to please someone else.

KLEPTOMANIA (Stealing)	Your soul is saying that you want spiritual knowledge but you misinterpret it as wanting material possessions. You do not understand that you have it all inside you.
POSTERIA - LARGE	Sitting on your wants! Holding on to concepts that stop you going after what you want.
SCIATICA	You are disregarding your own wants. Therefore not communicating to yourself and others what you want for yourself.
(When Pregnant)	Thinking of baby's wants and not of your own.
URINE - OFFENSIVE	Stagnant, not going after your wants. It is offensive to you.
URINE - RETENTION	Holding on to the concept that you cannot have what you want.

CHAPTER 10

CHAKRA No 3
REPRODUCTIVE AREA - NEEDS

THE CONCEPT TO KEEP IT HEALTHY IS "ONE WITH ALL"

"COMPETITION" WILL CAUSE TROUBLE IN ALL
REPRODUCTIVE ORGANS

The following are the five **needs** which are essential for a fulfilling life, plus the **organs** associated with each need, also the **concept** that keeps them healthy.

FOOD	UTERUS or PROSTATE	**GROWTH**
HEALTH	SEXUAL IMPULSE or LIBIDO	**ENTHUSIASM**
SHELTER	OVARIES or SCROTUM or TESTICLES	**PROTECTION**
LOVE	VAGINA or PENIS	**TEACHING**
SEX	OVUM or SPERM (SEMEN)	**COMMUNICATION**

To keep the energy for this chakra flowing smoothly, it is the feeling of being **one with all**.

The minute you stop this one with God and the universe feeling, you are separated. The minute you think you are separated you are into competition and competition stops you from obtaining your needs. When you cannot obtain your needs, you have stress and you become a "poor little me" and you start bitching and moaning and blaming others.

This stress plays a major role in causing your body to store energy instead of letting it flow through as it is supposed to. Not wanting a need will also put pressure on you. Your soul knows what you need, but you are "fighting" it. The reason may be due to a fear of some sort.

Competition takes all the pleasure out of doing things. It just causes pressure, especially if you start competing against yourself. Either way, you are not doing it for yourself, which is the only way to enjoy the doing.

To be one with all, means that you are not thinking that you are lesser than anyone or that you are greater than anyone.

Be decisive and creative with your energy and know that you have the power to use all your resources to obtain all your needs.

"The Thrill Is Not Just In The Winning But
The Courage To Join The Race."

69

Both spiritual and physical natures of each need, needs to be taken into account and balanced.

Being **one with all** is the overall learning experience for this chakra but as you see, for each need there is a separate learning experience. So, if you are having trouble with any of these organs, it could be that you are not doing the positive concept for either the spiritual side or the physical side.

Here is the way to keep these organs healthy:-

1. FOOD - UTERUS or PROSTATE - GROWTH

SPIRITUAL

"Food for thought" is your need here.growth from the understanding of regrouping yourself or reading books for spiritual growth or attending self awareness building classes to start living what you have learned and raise your level of consciousness. When there is no intake of spiritual food and changing ways from being dogmatic about thinking that my way is best or being critical of others, there is a big chance that you will suffer from either a prolapsed uterus or an enlarged prostate gland.

PHYSICAL

The food you eat needs to be enjoyable and containing all the nutrients needed for the growth and maintenance of your body.

2 HEALTH - SEXUAL IMPULSE or LIBIDO - ENTHUSIASM

SPIRITUAL

The need here is to be enthusiastic for a spiritual life, such as, love yourself and have faith in yourself. Find your purpose and follow your feelings.

PHYSICAL

Keep your enthusiasm for your life in the physical by being involved by doing for yourself so you can then do for others. Always know why you are doing things and never feel greater or lesser than others.

"Words Kill More Than Guns."

3. SHELTER - OVARIES or SCROTUM or TESTICLES - PROTECTION

SPIRITUAL

This need is to feel secure inside and knowing you have a team of Master Souls to help you get through this lifetime, so use them. Ask for help, meditate to feel cool, calm and collected and confident. Have the inner authority to make and keep boundaries to be solid inside.

PHYSICAL

This need is to have a roof over your head and a place to call your own where you can protect your family and nurture your children. A place where you can be protected when you go to sleep.

4. LOVE - VAGINA or PENIS - TEACHING .....

SPIRITUAL

This need is to show that you are love and by just being the love that you are, you are being an example to others. Simply teaching what you know by saying what you feel. By teaching what you know, you can gain more for yourself. Your children choose you, for the knowledge you have in you to teach them. Your good or not so good vibrations of your concepts that you give off, are picked up by your children and others. Children particularly, because they are so sensitive as they are only using their feelings. e.g.: If the parent is not secure in himself, the child will pick that up and will feel insecure also.

The minute the soul attaches itself to the body forming in the womb, you teach it by your behavior. The baby picks up all your feelings and emotions. If the baby feels it is not going to be given enough love for it's needs from either parent, it decides to leave. (This is a cause of a miscarriage, a stillborn child or a cot death). A child needs unconditional, one with all, deep feeling love, not just the romantic type love.

Parents need to just be their love and not be vying between each other for their child's love. This competition puts pressure on these parents' organs and will breed competition and confusion in the child.

"An Acorn Is As Perfect As A Fully Grown Oak Tree."

PHYSICAL

Find your **inner essence** and be it, so that you live it and give it out so others can see it and learn from it.

People are sensitive to the tone of your voice. This could be the reason why sometimes your love is not taken in the way it was meant.

Take the time to explain to little children why you are doing the things you are doing to them. Then you will not give them so many blocks, fears or traumas. You were little once! Remember, children are old souls in new bodies.

Love your enemies and they will not be your enemies any more! If you are on the receiving end of some abuse, just take it in and transmute that negative energy into love energy and say thankyou for that energy or else convert it into love and send it back to the giver and the abuse will decrease.

5. SEX - OVUM or SPERM (SEMEN) - COMMUNICATION

SPIRITUAL

This is the need to communicate with your inner self and your inner Guidance to feel at one with yourself and others and the world and the universe.

You need this communication with your inner self to find the solutions to why you do the things you do and how you need to change for the better.

You also need to communicate to yourself what your purpose and your direction is for this lifetime.

PHYSICAL

If you have been taught somehow, that the opposite sex is either greater or lesser than you, you will have trouble with relationships with the opposite sex. It could even lead to not being able to have children.

You need to know each sex has it's role to play and is no better than the other and you need to work as a team.

The more people you communicate with, the more you can learn for yourself. That raises your level of consciousness which is your need.

The reasons that could stop that communication is thinking you are better than others. -- (who wants to be with that sort of person?) or thinking you are lesser than others -- (little mice or "door mats", just get walked over). Knowing that you are one with all is the answer.

"No Communication Causes Confusion Which Leads To Conflict."

You learn to be creative and use your potential when you need to deal with different situations with the opposite sex.

* * * * * * * * *

Do you see now that your power comes from understanding the spiritual nature of your five physical needs? This power of understanding starts you spiralling upwards through the higher spiritual chakras and keeps life simple and enjoyable with peace and harmony.

"If You Are At Peace With Yourself,
You Will Discern Peace Around You."
Sri Sathya Sai Baba

AILMENTS	YOUR ATTITUDES THAT STOP YOUR ENERGY FLOW THROUGH YOUR REPRODUCTIVE AREA

BULIMIA

food - growth - spiritual

You are needing spiritual growth, which you do not understand how to obtain, so you have this hunger and you over eat and it is not what you need, so you throw it up.

CANDIDA ALBICANS (Thrush) *(For overall thought as well See Chakra No 2)*

shelter - protection - spiritual

• In your ovaries, you **doubt** that you can protect yourself spiritually.

love - teaching - spiritual

• In your vagina, you **doubt** that you have anything to give.

love - teaching - physical

• In the vagina, **doubting** self. Thinking that you are lesser than men - feel at one with everyone.

• Bloating is the accumulation of any of these concepts.

CHILDBIRTH PAIN

love - teaching - physical

It is your choice to have this pain. There is no need for this pain. Your muscles are affected by **guilt** and that guilt is from greater than or lesser than thoughts. Some women feel immense power over their husbands at their ability to bear children. Then others feel guilt at having to carry out this function. It is your choice to have this guilt and suffer. There is also a nutritional factor that has lowered our general level of health on this planet. This additional stress and strain becomes extremely painful to what is an essentially natural function.

COMPULSIVE
EATING

food - growth - spiritual

You are being drawn to eating too much because
you need spiritual growth. Maybe you are not
putting your knowledge into practise.

CRAB LICE
(Pediculus Pubis)

love - teaching - physical

You have attracted these parasitic lice because
you are not giving out your spiritual knowledge
and this "irritates" you. Teach what you know,
and pass it on always. Do not think that you
know it all and wait till others have to ask you
what you know. You are nurturing lice instead
of nurturing people!

EDOMETRIOSIS
(Uterus)

S *food - growth - spiritual*

Your need is to grow spiritually, (see page 6 for 10
ways to do it) so you have a new approach to your
life. Understand yourself and remove old limiting
concepts.

ENDOMETRITIS
(Uterus)

food - growth - physical

Stirred up emotions of not wanting to change old
ideas and learn new ones. The competition is
thinking that other people know more than you
do and you cannot learn like they can or you
think you know better.

GENITAL HERPES
(Simplex virus)
(Vagina or penis)

love - teaching - physical

If you are not allowing yourself to be the **love**
that you are, you will not be at peace with
yourself so your immune system ceases to work
and the virus attacks.

IMPOTENCE
(Erectile insufficiency)
(Libido)

health - enthusiasm - physical

A fear of some sort from the past is stopping you
feel at one with your sexual feelings and you
think you are lesser than others.

MENOPAUSE (Hot flushes)	*love - teaching - physical* At puberty, a young girl wonders why does this have to happen to me? At menopause time, a woman thinks the same thing. Her thoughts go to why should this be happening to me, and why am I not in control of my own body? This thought of not wanting to be told, causes all the hot flushes of temperature.
MENSTRUATION FLOODING (Vagina)	*love - teaching - physical* Competing against someone for someone else's love.
MENSTRUATION PAINS (Vagina)	*love - teaching - physical* Competing for outside love. Your need is to love yourself and to know that the love you are looking for is inside you. When you live your love, you are an example to others. Where there is love there is no pain.

OBESITY AFTER CHILDBIRTH

sex - communication - spiritual

- You need more communication with your inner self to see what concepts you are holding on to and need to discard.

- Holding on to thoughts of not wanting this baby and not communicating it to anyone.

sex - communication - physical

- You are thinking you are lesser than your husband. You need equality in communication.

food - growth - physical

- Eating too much but the food you are needing is for your own spiritual growth of becoming enlightened to whom you really are - a soul with a physical body - not a physical body with a soul. Finding your purpose and developing a live and let live attitude. Letting go of judging and blaming etc. *(See Page 6)*

PREMATURE EJACULATION	*sex - communication - spiritual*

You are thinking you are greater than your partner. Therefore, not treating girls as equal. You are not communicating to yourself, your need to be one with all. You do not realize that you both need to gain pleasure from this union and that is giving up the thought that you are greater than she is.

sex - communication - physical

- Competition. I've got to be the best or the first always.

- You must do this quickly because you should not be doing this. (Thoughts from your youth.)

- Not being in control of your own needs.

PRE MENSTRUAL TENSION   *love - teaching - spiritual*

Fear of living, so you are not living your love.

PROSTATE GLAND ENLARGED   *food - growth - spiritual*

Needs spiritual growth to change and grow from your old dogmatic ways of thinking that my way is best or critical of others.

PROSTATITIS   *food - growth - spiritual*

Stirred up emotions of competition that stops your growth.

THRUSH in Vagina   *love - teaching - physical*

Thinking you are lesser or greater than men. Feel at one with everyone.

UTERUS PROLAPSED   *food - growth - spiritual*

Needs spiritual growth to change and grow from your old dogmatic ways of thinking that my way is best or critical of others.

CHAPTER 11

CHAKRA No 4 - SOLAR PLEXUS - IDENTITY

THE CONCEPT TO KEEP IT HEALTHY IS "POSITIVITY"

"NEGATIVITY" WILL CAUSE TROUBLE IN: **PANCREAS, SPLEEN, STOMACH, LIVER, GALL BLADDER** and **SMALL INTESTINE,** (DUODENUM, JEJUNUM, ILEUM)

THE POSITIVE CONCEPT FOR EACH ORGAN IS:

PERSONAL:

PANCREAS	SUCCESS
SPLEEN	SINCERITY
STOMACH	UNDERSTANDING
LIVER	LEARNING
GALL BLADDER	BEINGNESS

BUSINESS:

DUODENUM	EMPATHY
JEJUNUM	KNOWING
ILEUM.	HONESTY

Knowing who you are, where you came from, why you are here and where you are going stops you worrying. Your maturity comes from the realization that you are a spiritual being with a physical body who has come to planet earth to learn and **grow** from your physical wants and needs. (the lower chakras). When you **change** to this understanding of your identity, you become **positive** and you use your **feelings.** When you are guided by your feelings, you relax and restore yourself to your **beingness.**

The state of being is simply being yourself, your true feelings, your true identity, without all the limitations of fears that we have accumulated over the centuries. This is the way you were as a child. This is the way of the dolphins.

Beingness is the positive concept to keep the gall bladder healthy. When you just accept that this offensive bile **just is** and that it is like it is because of it's **function** and you stop calling it offensive, you are just letting things **be** - that is beingness.

If you think people and objects are offensive, you have thoughts of bitterness toward them. That is what will crystalize in your gall bladder and cause gall stones.

When you stop living in the present moment and stop being in your feelings, your old memories come to the surface and stop you from being. This is why regrouping yourself is so necessary to find the solutions to why you do the things you do that sabotage your success.

"Winners Are Grinners. Losers Are Not Being Themselves."

You need love and empathy for yourself while you grow. Do not give yourself a hard time.

Likes and dislikes cause your system to be alkaline and worry causes it to be acid. Worry will sap your energy. In fact, all your ailments drain your energy. It is all your negative concepts. This thought pollution is the cause of all other pollutions on the planet and it is your body that suffers the most.

There is always a solution to every problem. You have all the help you need inside you. You just need to ask for it. Know that you are never alone.

This chakra needs to be positive by firstly being sincere with yourself to understand and learn. With this change you will have success in your **PERSONAL** growth.

For your **BUSINESS**, you need **empathy, knowing** and **honesty**. If you have these qualities for yourself you will have them for others.

All this positivity brings **maturity**. Wallowing in self-pity, enjoying your suffering and being governed by society's traditions are all negative reactions to keep you from your true feelings.

Nations and people who are repressed and have a lot of unrest in their countries and have little self-respect, usually make beautiful music. This is because they are not able to do what they want to, so it is **a way of expressing their inability of what they could be.**

Strive to know yourself more and just be yourself.

"When People Stop Worrying They Will Have More Energy."

80

AILMENTS	YOUR ATTITUDES THAT STOP YOUR ENERGY FLOW THROUGH YOUR SOLAR PLEXUS AREA
ALCOHOLISM	Lack of communication with others and worrying about it. Your feelings are hurt because no one values your presence. Alcohol relaxes your ligaments and you lose control of them. When you cannot control yourself, another person is controlled to look after you and take notice of you. Your liver is affected because you will not learn to control yourself.
ANOREXIA NERVOSA (Fear of becoming fat and refusing food)	Not understanding that you are living other people's standards. You are not using your power to be free and not be restricted by other people's ideas. Not getting your food needs leads to trouble in your uterus. *(see chakra 3)* You need the spiritual understanding of knowing yourself and start maturing to love yourself. If you do not know how to love yourself and be yourself, your soul wants to leave. (self-destruction)
BLOATED	Accumulation of your emotions in your small intestine. Therefore, no empathy, knowing or honesty or anything to do with your business.
CHICKEN POX (Herpes Zoster virus)	Children may have been let down or left out or not acknowledged and they have thoughts of unworthiness recurring.
CHOLESTEROL	You are wanting to hold on to what you have and you are wanting more.
DIABETES MELLITUS	The pancreas needs success. You cannot be a success if you are **ashamed** of yourself from something you did in the past. You **do not want to live** because of that emotion. You do not have a good relationship with yourself. (KIDNEYS) You do not want to see the future (CATARACTS) Self-destruction because of your direction if toes or what doing if fingers. (GANGRENE)

Continued ...

81

DIABETES *Continued*

Not doing things because you are a perfectionist. (HARDENING OF THE ARTERIES)

Not changing carbohydrates into glucose for energy for the brain to function. (WEIGHT LOSS)

DRUG ADDICTION

You feel negative about yourself and insecure about doing for yourself. You are seeking attention and hoping the person whom you want to love you will be affected by your actions against yourself. It continues because the person whom you want to love you does not realize that the way to really love someone is to give them responsibility to do for themselves. You have had too much done for you and that has made you weak and made you feel incapable. You have lost control of yourself so you need to learn to control yourself.

FLATULENCE

Turbulence of mixed up emotions of worry or turmoil inside. Not understanding the reasons for these emotions. *(See concepts of small and large intestines)*

GALL BLADDER

You are letting something stop your beingness. Everything has a specific function. **Beingness** embraces it and lets it be.

GALL STONES

You are not allowing yourself to just **be** yourself because of some bitterness towards somebody or something. This negativity crystallizes when you are not letting others **be** themselves. When your **beingness** is in evidence you allow others to be the same.

HEARTBURN

Not regrouping your experiences and worrying about not **understanding** what has happened to you.

HEPATITIS A

You have allowed your feelings to be hurt and now you do not want to **learn** anything about yourself. Your **liver** is kept healthy by your growth from learning from everything you do. You have to learn to be yourself in any situation and let other people be themselves as well. In other words, keep in your own energy.

HIATUS HERNIA   You are guilty of not understanding what you need to do and you worry about it.

HICCOUGHS   You need to think more about your feelings and be jolted into using them and understanding them.

HICCOUGHS   Missed opportunity to use your feelings.
From indigestion

HYPERGLYCAEMIA (Pancreas is not secreting enough insulin therefore too much sugar in the blood.)

The **pancreas** needs you to be a **success.** If you have thoughts of being **ashamed** of yourself you **resign** yourself to not being a success and just give in. **You do not know what to do** to stop this emotion from keeping you from moving on and forgetting the past and forgiving yourself. Your inner authority is the power you seek.

HYPOGLYCAEMIA (Over secretion of insulin by the Pancreas so there is a low level of sugar in the blood which the brain needs for it's energy. This can cause coma - unconsciousness. You need to eat more carbohydrates often.)

The **pancreas** needs you to be **successful** and if you have done something to make you **ashamed** of yourself, you cannot be successful but **you pressure yourself** to be a success but your ashamed thoughts stop you so you pick faults in people and things so you think that will make you think you are successful.

INDIGESTION #1   Missed opportunity of not **understanding** a situation and learning from it.

INDIGESTION #2   When your food seems to be "sitting on your stomach." you are not **understanding** what to do or how to do it when or where or why. Just not being able to move on.

INDIGESTION #3   Not digesting food is not **understanding** that you need to live for yourself.

JAUNDICE	You are not just **being** and letting others just be. This **beingness** is loving yourself which you need to **learn**.
JAUNDICED NEW BORN BABIES	Liver is for **learning** and the baby is coming to learn to heal the situation from it's past lifetime with it's new parent. The baby is experiencing pressure from a fear of confronting this person again.
LIVER	You are not **learning** about why you allow others to hurt your feelings.
MORNING SICKNESS	Wanting to rid yourself of any of these thoughts :-

- Fear of Pain from previous lifetimes causes hormone secretion which is unable to be digested.
- Thoughts from other lifetimes bubble up and you want to get rid of them.
- I do not think I will be doing what I want to do from now on.

MOTION SICKNESS	The overall cause is you are wanting to get rid of some fears that stop you from being in your feelings - such as:- "I will not be able to swim to safety from this boat" or "I am unable to get out of this vehicle" etc.
MUCOUS MEMBRANE	Understanding.
NAUSEA	Not **understanding** the situation so you have mixed up emotions.
PANCREAS	You are not **successful** because you hide your feelings through being **ashamed** of something you have done.
PERISTALSIS (Involuntary motion to propel contents of intestines, etc.)	If you are not being your true **feelings** you will affect this action.

POST VIRAL **FATIGUE** **SYNDROME**	When a virus attacks you, it is because you have let a certain concept weaken your body and the virus has been able to take over in the weakened area. The trouble is, you have not regrouped yourself after the illness and worked out exactly why you became ill. If you do not do this, you are liable to have the disease recur.
	Secondly, when you do not regroup, you get tired because you cannot move on without understanding yourself, so you just stay tired with sore muscles which indicates guilt. A nervous headache indicates no communication with yourself. It is a must to understand your experiences.
PYLORIC **STENOSIS**	**CONGENITAL -** You do not want to have anything to do with business this lifetime due to thoughts from a past lifetime.
	WHEN OLD DUE TO CANCER You would rather die than do business.
SHINGLES **Herpes Zoster**	A recurring problem of unworthiness brought on by stress, therefore no peace to keep your **virus** immune system working so the virus from having had chicken pox can flare up and cause this rash and pain.
SMALL **INTESTINE**	These three are parts of your small intestine and you need **empathy**, **knowing** and **honesty** for your **business** life.
- DUODENUM	You have no **empathy** for self or others.
- JEJUNUM	You have not obtained all the facts to **know** what you are doing to be secure.
- ILEUM	You are not being **honest** with self or others.
	ULCERS in any of these areas means you are holding on to these concepts for too long.
SPLEEN	Not being **sincere** with yourself and others by not loving yourself or others or both.

STOMACH	You are not taking the time to **understand** the things you do so you can grow to feel positive.
STOMACH ULCERS	Holding on to the concept of worrying and putting pressure on yourself. You are not loving or respecting yourself to **understand** why you are doing that to yourself.
THEFT FROM YOU	• You are not being honest with yourself. • You are being too possessive.
VOMITING	I want to get rid of these emotions.

CHAPTER 12

CHAKRA No 5 - HEART - DRIVE

THE CONCEPT TO KEEP IT HEALTHY IS:
"DEVOTION TO SELF"

"OUTSIDE DEVOTION" WILL CAUSE TROUBLE IN

THYMUS, HEART, CIRCULATORY SYSTEM, BREASTS, LUNGS, DIAPHRAGM, LYMPHATIC SYSTEM and IMMUNE SYSTEM.

The heart chakra is where your expression of love begins. Your **heart** is the pump for your **circulatory** system and **love** is it's driving force. From understanding who you are, in your solar plexus, you can see that being devoted to yourself first is the next step to raising your consciousness. Inner motivation is what gives you incentive and enthusiasm. Outer motivation from being devoted to a parent, a spouse, a child, your business or organization will sap all your enthusiasm. Unless you are gaining some understanding or learning from it, you will not love what you are doing. On the other hand, when you do for yourself and know why you are doing it, you will follow through and accomplish with ease.

If you do it **your way** you will keep your lungs healthy. Every time you ask a child to do something, simply tell the child **what** you want done, not **how** you want it done. Let the child use it's own creativity. If you force your way on to others, they cannot enjoy the doing. Then you wonder why children will not do anything for you. There is no enthusiasm when you are not allowed to do things the way you want to do them.

The **diaphragm** is the pump for your **lymphatic** system and **harmony** is it's driving force.

My lymphatic system was "shot to ribbons" and I had very little harmony inside me. (I could pretend on the outside), I was always yearning for friends and always felt a failure. You are only a failure if you think you are a failure!

When I changed to loving myself and feeling better about myself, it brought about such a difference in me, that now I have many wonderful friends.

One friend in particular wrote to me saying that he has a machine for healing the lymphatic system and that my book has made the necessary addition for complete healing.

I find this Lymphaciser machine to be the most valuable tool for healing to the cell level. Combined with loving thoughts and understanding to be in harmony with yourself and others, you will bring forth a very healthy body.

"Nothing Is Achieved Without Enthusiasm"

This New Zealand Rainbow RH 48 Body Energiser improves circulation of the cleansing lymph. It brings the oxygen level up. This removes toxins via lungs, sinuses, skin, bowel and kidneys.

The unique controlled breath approach improves your breath range so as to clean the Central Nervous System. With the posture change, it allows more energy for a better attitude. So with thinking positively, drinking purified water and a good diet, you have a family in-home self healing.

For a see, hear and feel Video and Info Pak on this Body Energiser contact:
    Mr. LYMPHACISER
    www.ourlifeforce.com
    EMAIL ian@ourlifeforce.com

Your devotion to self and love of self brings about the harmony you need inside you. You will find that once you start loving yourself, you will have a lot more friends who want to be near you. Because you are enjoying yourself, you attract others who want to do the same.

Peace is the concept of the **immune system**. Now you can see that love, harmony and peace is what keeps your body full of energy. Your immune system and your lymphatic system both have to do with your blood or circulatory system and those three concepts **Love, Harmony** and **Peace** give each **cell** in your body the **power** to function.

Is it not obvious that all your non loving concepts cause **toxins** in your body which simply **give away your power?**

An idea to put some energy back into your cells is to think of the loveliest thing that has ever happened to you. Close your eyes and imagine yourself putting that thought into your heart and let it flow through all your arteries out to each organ through your body or to a certain area that needs attention.

Your **thymus** is to **activate your love for yourself.** When you are doing for yourself it is being called upon to act and help you do it. It is no where if it is not being used. When you are loving yourself, it is in the centre of your chest. Because your love is the most powerful force, you need to use it to your advantage **all the time**, not just sometimes. It will help you do everything so easily when you live your love and be loyal to yourself.

If you are feeling that you will not be able to do something, trust your love inside that you will. When you are doing for yourself, you are loving yourself.

"Negative Thoughts Are Just Energy.
Simply Transmute Them To Love Energy For Yourself."

SOME WAYS TO LOVE YOURSELF

- Acknowledge your divinity and your beauty.
- Take note of what you say and what you think about yourself. Eliminate those put downs such as "I am a clumsy idiot" Say instead, "That was a silly thing to do". Put aggression towards the incident instead of towards yourself.
- Laugh at yourself but not in a derogatory way.
- You are No 1. Put yourself first always.
- Spend time doing what you really want to do for yourself.
- Focus on your spiritual and physical **needs** before your wants.
- Follow through on a project.
- Do not waste time on trivia.
- Learn from everything you do without judging yourself.
- Throw out old possessions.
- Always know what you want, so others can not tell you.
- Be loyal to yourself and always make goals.
- State what your boundaries are, so people respect you.
- Take time to meditate and relax.
- Do things for yourself that you do not usually do.
- Buy something for yourself that you would not buy before.
- Let go of authority figures. Stand up for yourself.
- Look at the beauty around you - the trees and parks.
- Keep your home tidy for yourself.
- Take more care with your clothing.
- Take more care with what you eat.
- Ask a friend to list your five good qualities.
- Think of someone you admire and write their good qualities that you see in them. You then know that you have those qualities in you because you could not see them otherwise.

People who love themselves do NOT take drugs.

"The Most Wasted Of All Days Is That On Which One Has Not Laughed"
- Nicolas Chamfort

AILMENTS -   **YOUR ATTITUDES THAT STOP**
YOUR ENERGY FLOW THROUGH
YOUR HEART CHAKRA AREA.

ANAEMIA   Not loving yourself. Devotion to someone else
(Iron deficiency)   and you are possessive.

ANAEMIA   You cannot understand that you must love
(Pernicious)   yourself in spite of what others think about you.
                     Loving yourself gives you peace.

AQUIRED   Whatever area you have weakened by your
IMMUNE   negative thoughts against yourself, that is where
DEFICIENCY   the virus will strike you. The negative thoughts
SYNDROME   are anything that stops you having inner **peace**
(A.I.D.S.)   for your **immune system** to give up it's
                     defence. So, make sure that you are involved,
                     successful and fulfilled in your life to stop those
                     wars inside you that are not peace. Peace only
                     comes when you have the inner authority to be
                     yourself and love yourself no matter what
                     anyone thinks. Letting yourself be controlled by
                     what society thinks about you, does not allow you
                     to have inner peace. If you have hurt feelings
                     that you allow yourself to stop loving yourself,
                     you will never have inner peace. If you are only
                     thinking of the physical and materialistic side of
                     life and not growing spiritually, you are not
                     doing your soul's plan. So what is the use of
                     being here if you are not at peace.

ASTHMA   It starts in your No. 1 Chakra - Self-Acceptance .
                     You are not being satisfied with yourself, and
                     that is your running nose. Then it goes to your
                     chest area. By not being satisfied, you start
                     doing things that are not in your best interest and
                     driving yourself to do things that your parents
                     think you "should" do so that people will notice
                     you. Doing things the way others want you to.
                     When you cannot breathe, you are not enjoying
                     life because you are not being devoted to
                     yourself.

DIFFICULTY BREATHING IN - Not loving yourself
                     enough to enjoy life.

DIFFICULTY BREATHING OUT - Not able to give your
                     love with ease.

BLOOD	When you change your perception of loving yourself, your haemoglobin deteriorates. (Blood needs love) (Pigment is your perception of yourself)
	Your perception of things needs to be positive. Simply embrace the things you consider bad. In loving all things and perceiving them as all having a function, you could eliminate all harmful substances from your body. Your white cells would not need to fight.
BREAST (Cancer)	Not nurturing yourself. Doing for others before you.
BREAST FEEDING (Inability)	You cannot relax because:-

You cannot relax because:-
- You thought you would be tied down to the child all the time and you would not have your freedom.
- You are repulsed by the thought of breast feeding.
- You are holding on to fears of not being a good mother.
- You did not want to be a mother.
- You have a fear of no belief that you can do it.

BREASTS FLAT CHESTED	Not nurturing others with what others need.
BREASTS LARGE	Nurturing everybody else's needs.
BREAST TUMOUR	Not trusting yourself that you can nurture yourself.
BRONCHITIS	Stirred up emotions of not doing things your way. You want to get rid of the thought that you are not in charge.
CHEST CONGESTED	Submission or giving in to someone's wishes. Not allowing yourself to do things your way.
CIRCULATORY SYSTEM	Not motivating yourself by loving yourself **Love** is your driving force. The **blood** needs pure love of self. Putting yourself down or hating what you do is the energy that goes against your life force.

EMPHYSEMA	You are not doing things your way. Doing what others say is right for you because you are not devoted to yourself and doing for yourself first. Not able to be yourself.
FROZEN SHOULDERS (Muscles)	Not shouldering your **responsiblity.**
Left Shoulder	**Guilt** is stopping you from being responsible to understand yourself so that you can just be yourself.
Right Shoulder	**Guilt** is causing you to not take responsibility to gain for yourself from what ever you do.
HAEMOPHILIA (Impaired coagulation in blood)	From a past lifetime that you have done things that stop you loving yourself. You need to forgive yourself and start loving yourself so you have giving and taking - love and greed in balance.
HEART	**Love** yourself by doing for yourself, because you are No 1, then you will have the drive to be successful,
HEART - BLOCKAGE	Caring more for others than yourself and not living for yourself and not doing for yourself first. You are blocking off yourself and what you are living for. You are not finding your purpose to start living it.
HEART - ENLARGED	Big hearted! Doing everything to please others.
HYPERTENSION (High blood pressure)	Saying "that person makes my blood boil" means you are allowing that person to rule your life, instead of finding a way to heal those emotions. Any continuing pressure from a situation stops you flowing with your own feelings. You are letting your emotions and reactions rule you. If you are **doing for yourself** and minding your own business and let other people get on with their own lives, then your heart would be beating at your own pace.
HYPOTENSION (Low blood pressure)	You are not loving yourself because of outside devotion. When you are not doing for yourself, you lose enthusiasm and drive.

| IMMUNE SYSTEM | Any thoughts that go against your inner **peace** breaks down your defences. Change your ways to love yourself and see the good in yourself and others. Following your feelings and not your intellect. Being in control of your own life, is the spiritual growth that brings you peace of mind. |

INFLUENZA
(Aching muscles)

Not wanting to do what someone else has told you to do and being **guilty** about it.

CHEST CONGESTED)
COUGHING)
HEADACHE)
NOSE RUNNING)
SNEEZING)   *See Common Cold*
TEMPERATURE)   *Chapter*
THROAT - LOSS OF VOICE)
THROAT - PHLEGM)
THROAT - SORE)

LUNGS

Make sure you are **doing things your way.**

LUNG CANCER

Self destruction. Not being devoted to yourself enough to resist others telling you how to do things. Giving in and doing things their way.

LYMPHATIC SYSTEM

Any negative thoughts against yourself creates disharmony. **Harmony** is gained by learning from your anxieties and bringing balance into your physical and spiritual life.

NIPPLES - RETRACTED

You do not want to give out your **nurturing**.

NIPPLES - SORE OR CRACKED

The outlet that gives out your **nurturing**.

- Thinking you are not good enough.
- You do not like doing it.
- You do not think the other person is good enough to be nurtured.

PLEURISY

The pleura is the serum that **lubricates** in between the lungs and the rib cage. So **enthusiasm** is what keeps it lubricated. Do it your way with enthusiasm. Do what you want or like or what is best for you.

PNEUMONIA

Stirred up emotions of being told how to do things and you do not want to change from being devoted to someone else.
(See Shallow Breathing)   Continued....

CHEST - CONGESTED	)	
COLD SORES	)	*See Common Cold*
COUGHING	)	*Chapter*
TEMPERATURE	)	

REACTION TO
DEODORANT   No feelings for self.

SHALLOW
BREATHING   Not living life to the fullest.

SNORING   Rebelling at what you are regrouping for
yourself in the universe - not being devoted to
self.

TOXINS   You are giving away your power by having any
(In blood and lymph)   negative thoughts against yourself. (blood needs
love)(lymph needs harmony)

WHEEZING   Complaining that you can not be yourself.

CHAPTER 13

CHAKRA No 6 - THYROID - RELATING

THE CONCEPT TO KEEP IT HEALTHY IS "COMPASSION"

"JUDGMENTAL" WILL CAUSE TROUBLE IN: **THYROID, PARATHYROIDS, TONSILS, THROAT, LARYNX, PHARYNX. PAROTID GLANDS AND SALIVARY GLANDS (SUBMAXILLARY)**

This thyroid chakra is where you relate to others. When you are loving yourself, you can show compassion for yourself, then it naturally flows to others. This compassion for self and others is you being in your true feelings and that is the real you.

This is where you need to be relaxed when dealing with people, so you can relate with ease. The pressure you feel about your neck area can be from worrying about what other people are thinking about you. Remember, we are all in the same boat!

You communicate more non verbally than verbally and how you feel about a person is how you relate to them. This chakra is where you form your opinions of what you will actually speak out in your next chakra, which is your outflow.

Judging, is the opposite to compassion and judging will hurt you more than it will harm the person you are judging. Your throat will suffer when you judge others or you cannot relate to another's actions or attitudes. The same applies if you judge yourself.

Jealousy is the main reason for judging people, because people are always looking outside of themselves instead of realizing that they have everything inside them.

A **live and let live attitude** is required here. Be yourself always when with others and let others have their opinions. You will not be their friend for long if you do not. Focus on people's good points for your own good.

If you or others are being "stiff-necked", stubborn or inflexible, just evaluate the situation without judging and move on.

"Desire Not To Please Others. Desire To Be Pleasant To Others"
- Saint Germain

9 5

Understand others by putting yourself in other people's shoes. Always look to see what **you** have done or not done before you blame someone. It is just another way to be compassionate. It is far better to generate loving thoughts than to show hate and anger because whatever you put out, the same will be returned to you.

We are all here to help each other and learn from each other. Why is it that we cannot relate to some people and others we have no trouble with at all? When you have the ability to live and let live, you will see that it is beneficial to look inside and work out the reason for you not being able to relate to somebody and then resolve the matter so you can be at ease with yourself and others.

"Enemies Are A Projection Of That Which You Judge Of Yourself"
- Saint Germain

AILMENTS -	YOUR ATTITUDES THAT STOP YOUR ENERGY FLOW THROUGH YOUR THYROID AREA.
CHOKING	You are not relating to what you think is right for you.
MUMPS (Parotid Glands)	Someone has judged you and you cannot relate to it. You need to be solid in your personal with self confidence to be able to take criticism.
NECK STIFFNESS	You are judging others and yourself and not changing to a live and let live attitude because you are inflexible and not in your feelings.
SALIVARY GLAND (Sub-Maxillary)	You cannot relate to emotions that you have just stirred up. You are living in the past.
THROAT - PHLEGM	You cannot relate to someone from what they have said or done. You need a live and let live attitude.
THROAT - SORE	Being frustrated and not relating to yourself for not being able to have someone understand your point of view.
THROAT - TICKLE	You just cannot relate to something that you have done or not done. (In other words judging yourself.)
TONSILITIS	Judging the person you cannot relate to because some emotions have been stirred up. This could be yourself.

CHAPTER 14

CHAKRA No 7 - PITUITARY - OUTFLOW

THE CONCEPT TO KEEP IT HEALTHY IS "HUMILITY"

"GLORY" WILL CAUSE TROUBLE IN: EYES, VOCAL CORDS, MOUTH, FRONT OF BRAIN, THIRD EYE and UPPER TEETH.

This outflow chakra is where you **give out** your energy in different forms. Using your creativity to be of service in giving out the understanding of your inner essence. To have humility in doing this, means to just outflow as if I am one with you as I am one with myself. Not for the glory of doing it to be recognized and liked, but to simply **believe in what you do and say.**

With all the experiences you have had over the years from which you have learned, you need to **delegate** to others. They can then learn what you know and you are free to learn new things for yourself. While you are learning new things, you can help yourself to learn it by teaching it to others. As you teach what you need to learn, the more you say it to others, the more it makes an impression on your consciousness. This is being of service to you and to others.

From all the learning in your first 6 chakras, you need to give it out here in your **feelings**, which is the strength that keeps your back bone upright to **support yourself** and **stand up for yourself.** Always say and do what you feel. Do not let your **intellect** interfere with your outflow. It could think that you have to be perfect before you give your knowledge out.

Your intellect can be any emotion such as **guilt**, that you have not given enough or you are not good enough for something. This could impair your **muscles** that hold your spine erect. Forgive yourself and say you will do better next time and get back into your true feelings again.

There are all sorts of excuses that the intellect can come up with to stop you outflowing and saying or doing what you feel. Remember to stand up tall and give out what you need. This need, if not fulfilled will fill you with too much importance and thoughts of glory will puff you up.

Some people simply talk about what they could do, but that is as far as they go. These people miss out on those glorious feelings that come from being involved, feeling successful and feeling fulfilled.

If you are always in your feelings, you are the one who can take control of your life and change your destiny and make it what you want it to be. Without your intellect controlling you, you can outflow with authority and not let others control your life.

"Silence Is The Virtue Of Fools" - *Francis Bacon*

99

If you are about to do for others, make sure they have **asked** you for your help. Nobody needs to be saved by do-gooders. By doing for people who could be doing for themselves, you are being inconsiderate by taking away their opportunity to grow. Why do you think missionaries were boiled in the pot? Nobody asked them to force their beliefs on to others.

Always remember the Chinese proverb - "Why do you hate me when I have not helped you yet?"

If you are putting too much out without learning from it, you will deplete your energy.

A soul is happy when it keeps evolving, so you need to organize your time to outflow by applying your skills whether it be by sharing your knowledge by speech or actually performing a skill.

Your third eye has to do with your inner visions of your soul and it shows you the **direction** in which your soul needs to go. When your inner visions appear, they are for you to plan your outflow. When you do not understand these visions, you go against the soul's plan.

Your eyes are to see what you **already know.** You see it, so you can **recall** what you need to do. Your eyes are your **abundance.** You see what needs to be organized so your life can flow smoothly and live in the **present.**

Your **eyesight** deteriorates because you do not want to see how you waste time when all your outflow is concentrated on everything but the **present.**

TO LIVE IN THE PRESENT:- See your **direction** with your third eye. **Organize** your **time** so you can be **relaxed** and in your **feelings** to just **be** yourself, then you will **outflow with humility** from your feelings.

It is most important to be **married to the process** when you outflow what you know.

Whatever you have given out, **be divorced from the result.** If you have done your best, that is all that matters. Do not worry about the outcome.

When you are thinking positively in each of your chakras, there is no stored up energy to block the flow. Therefore energy flows smoothly through all of them to keep your body healthy.

"Dumb Are The Wise When They Can't
Make Anyone Understand Them."

Karen Cohen

ACCIDENTS   If you go around aimlessly, **without a purpose,** accidents will happen, so you will have something to regroup and work out why you had the accident. **Nothing is a co-incidence.** Everything happens for a purpose, even to just stubbing your toe. Your direction would need to be attended to in some way. *(See Bones Chart.)* You most probably were in the wrong place at the wrong time. The area where you are injured is where you need to do something about. Take note of the chakra and what you are or are not doing for that chakra.

COLOUR   Not seeing things as they are.
BLINDNESS

EYES   Not organizing your time so that you can **live in the present** always.

SOME CONCEPTS OF THE LEFT EYE:
- Not saying what you feel.
- Being fragmented and not concentrating on your needs.
- Not relaxed when outflowing.
- Not seeing good in things and criticizing as though you are better.
- Not seeing the big picture.
- Closing yourself from seeing the future.
- Showing your weakness when outflowing.

SOME CONCEPTS OF THE RIGHT EYE:
- Not liking the way you do things.
- You are being a perfectionist.
- Not doing things in time.
- Saying you cannot perform what needs to be done.
- Not outflowing what you know.
- Seeing what needs to be done but you cannot see how to do it.
- Thinking that good things do not happen to me.
- Knowing your ability and not doing anything with it.

EYES - **BAGS UNDER**	• Holding on to old concepts because you are not regrouping what you have done and learning from it all and then giving out that knowledge. When you give out your knowledge, you make it wisdom for yourself. • Holding on to the concept of not sharing what you know because you are waiting for people to come to you and ask for what you know. • Holding on to the concept of not sharing because others will know more than you.
EYES - **BLINKING** (Too much)	You run out of time and you do not want to see what you have not done. Because you were being racey, you have not planned and visualized your organization. Wasting time in between opportunities.
EYES - **CATARACT**	You are not seeing any future for yourself. You are not sharing your knowledge or skills which enables you to take in more new things.
EYES - **CONJUNCTIVITIS**	Stirred up emotions from seeing bad in things stops you from seeing the reality in things.
EYES - **GREY OR BLACK** **UNDERNEATH**	Not wanting to share your wisdom because you are afraid of what others will think of you.
EYES - **ITCHING**	Recurring problems of:- • Not being militant with your timing to achieve more. • Not thinking you are doing the things that are best for you. Not seeing what needs to be done. • Not thinking you are doing a good job.
EYES - **PTERYGUIM**	Not wanting to see other people's point of view - I know best!
EYES - STY	Stagnating - you are keeping thoughts of resentment for too long.
EYES - TIC **Left eyelid**	You are seeing bad in a lot of things, so this irritation is telling you that you think you are superior to others
Under left	You are telling yourself that what you have done is superior to others. *Continued....*

102

Right eyelid You want to be perfect, so you are cross with yourself because you have not done something perfectly. You tell yourself you are inferior.

Under right Scared that what you have done is not perfect or up to the standard required. Thinking other people's work will show you up as being inferior.

EYES - WATERING Not able to say what you want to say.

EYELIDS (Flakey skin) Not able to say what you feel because you think you are inadequate or unworthy.

EYELIDS (Protruding lower) You are resenting change. You do not want to say what you feel. (Read Zygomatic left and right in Bones Chart Chapter)

EYELIDS - RED The eye sees and you need to say the feeling of what you see and if you do not, the eyelid is put under pressure by some resentment which stops you from saying the feelings of what you see.

GROWING PAINS (Muscles) Thoughts of **guilt** from something you have done. Believe in what you do.

HAIR - GREYING (Front of head) (Hair is your insulation) (Pigment colour of hair is your perception of yourself) (Your Pituitary Gland needs to believe in what you do and say) When you stop believing in what you do and say, you are changing your perception of yourself and the pigment drains out of your hair.

HAIR - RECEDING (Forehead) (Hair serves as insulation and it grows in the skin which needs feelings of worthiness and being adequate.) If it stops growing at the front of your head, you are not insulating yourself with feelings of worth or being adequate. This does not allow you to see what needs to be done and outflow in your feelings.

HEADACHES (Front of head, pressure) Holding on to old limitations and not seeing good in anything. Thinking you are better than anyone else.

LIPS - CRACKED CORNERS	Frustrated. You are wanting to share more but you cannot because you think you may say the wrong thing.
LIPS - PARCHED	Frustrated with thinking you cannot impart your knowledge.
MIGRAINE (Nervous headache - Front of head)	• If you have something to hide, you do not want it **communicated.** • Not **communicating** with your inner being to know yourself. • Not believing you can stand up for yourself and **say** what you want. • Letting others tell you what to do and not **communicating** to them that you dislike being told what to do.
MOUTH	Thinking that you are not imparting your knowledge in a way you would like.
MOUTH - ULCERS	Stagnating, and keeping the habit too long, frustrated that you are not outflowing better than you are, when you cannot say what you feel.
PARKINSON'S DISEASE	The tremors are from not understanding a fear you have that stops you believing in what you do and say. So, you are not **communicating** to yourself that you teach what you need to learn when you give out your knowledge. Your **muscles** react to your **guilt** from not doing it.
PITUITARY GLAND	Not believing in what you do and say.
SINGING OUT OF TUNE	When you are not relating to people well, you are not in harmony with them or the universe. It then shows in your voice. Your voice sounds are vibrations of frequency and you need to upgrade your thinking to be one with all.
TEETH - (Upper Only)	You are not seeing the big picture of what the plan will be like when finished. *(For teeth detail see Chapter 6)* *(For lower teeth, see Chakra 1)*
TEETH - CLENCHED	You have a fear of some sort that is stopping you from believing in what you do or say.
TEETH - GRINDING	Fearful of doing your soul's plan.

TIREDNESS	<ul><li>Not planning and running out of time.</li><li>Being a perfectionist.</li><li>Outflowing your wisdom without taking in new learning. Giving too much without learning from it.</li><li>Doing something or not doing something that is going against the plan of your soul.</li><li>Not wanting to do your direction, so it is an escape.</li><li>Not regrouping or summing up what you have learned.</li><li>Not knowing how to communicate.</li></ul>
TONGUE - BITING	Either wanting to stop eating too much or wanting to stop saying too much.
TONGUE - BLOTCHES	Saying you do not impart your knowledge as well as others. Comparing - wanting to be better.
TONGUE - PIMPLES	Thinking you are inadequate with your sharing.
VOICE BOX (Loss of voice)	You think you know more than others, so it is a waste of time talking to them.

CHAPTER 15

AILMENTS THAT CAN BE ASSOCIATED WITH DIFFERENT CHAKRAS

AILMENTS	ATTITUDES THAT GO AGAINST YOU
ABSCESS (Pus in a cavity or tissue)	Stagnation. Holding on to an old concept. Emotions have festered because you are not using your creative inspirations to get out of old habits.
ACNE (Inflammation of the sebaceous **glands**)	Thinking that you do not want to face up to new things. **Living in the past**.
ALLERGY An abnormal response or reaction.	Who or what is annoying or aggravating you? Being emotional and not in your true feelings. You could be allergic to yourself and aggravated with what you are doing or not doing to or for yourself. You have not set boundaries for yourself.
ALLERGY - **YEAST**	You are allowing somebody to overpower you from being yourself. Make strong boundaries for yourself.
ARMS - **LEFT**	Not **doing** enough **spiritually** for yourself.
ARMS - **RIGHT**	**Physically** not **doing** enough for yourself. *(See Bones Chart)*
ARTERIES	**Perfectionism.**
ARTERIOSCLEROSIS (Thickening, and loss of elasticity in the walls of the arteries)	Worrying about not being **perfect** stops you from performing or doing.
ARTHRITIS - **OSTEO** Swollen, stiff, deformed, painful joints.	**Ligaments** - Not **controlling** yourself to do for yourself first. You have been taught to do for everyone else and to leave yourself out.

ARTHRITIS - **RHEUMATOID** Inflamed tissue, **tendons** **ligaments.** Red shiny skin over joints and as for Osteo.	**Immune** system needs **peace** to stop viral infections affecting these parts. Being **inflexible** and not in **control** can stop your peace within.
BACK ACHE	Your spinal column is for supporting you to stand up for yourself. Any thoughts such as resentment, guilt, inflexibility or not controlling yourself, are not your **true feelings**. Therefore indecisiveness between your true feelings and those previous intellectual, ego thoughts give you pain. *See the Bones Chart Chapter for the actual concept of the area you have the pain. Also which chakra is governing the area.*
BITES - **DOG OR** **SHARK**	Take note of where the bite is on your body. Blood pours out. You have attracted the animal to bite you because you are not loving yourself, so you put up your defences.
BITES - **MOSQUITOS,** **MIDGES,** **GNATS,** **FLIES**	A recurring problem, (itch) of being inadequate or unworthy (skin). Take note of where you are bitten.The bite is for you to love yourself more in some way because these insects suck your blood out therefore you are losing your love. Then, you can let an ailment into your blood such as:- dengue, malaria and Ross River fever and yellow fever if you are not loving yourself.
BITES - **SNAKE**	The snake secretes venom into you. You are not wanting to live.
BITES - **SPIDER**	Fever, (hot) not wanting to be told. (cold) not wanting to live.
BLEEDING	Letting go of your life force. "Bursting a blood vessel." Pushing yourself too hard to show that you are able to do things as well as others - proving yourself.
BLISTER	Cast off this habit that is irritating you.
BLOOD **BLISTER**	You are being agitated or pressured to cast off a bad habit.
BLOOD **CLOT**	A blockage of your energy flow. Fighting with the life force. Love is your driving force. You hate life because you do not realize you are here to learn from every experience.

108

BODY **ODOUR**	It is offensive to you and others when you are not in your **true feelings**. When you are fearful of anything such as public speaking. Not many people do not go into a cold sweat when facing a sea of people, but it is not you, it is some limitation that you have been taught into your intellect and you do not need it. The need for a deodorant when doing a sport is because you are competing, which takes you out of your feelings. (If you could simply play for yourself to improve your capabilities, you would be in your feelings).
BOIL **(Furuncle)** **CARBUNCLE** Larger than a boil with several openings.	Stirred up emotions that you have to let out because the stagnation of the concept has come to a head.
BONES	**Resentment** towards others or self. *(See Bones Chapter)*
BONES - **BREAKING**	Breaking point of not doing anything about the concept of **resentment**. Rebelling to the point of being brittle. Take note of the area of the break.*(see Bones Chapter)*
BONES - **CANCER**	**Resentment** is so strong that you do not want to change so it will destroy you. *(See Bones Chapter)*
BONES - **CRACKING**	Upper extremities - **resentment** causing friction in your doing. Lower extremities - **resentment** causing friction in your direction. "Lubricate" them with flexibility!
BRUISE	There is a need to look at your emotions towards a certain situation.
BUMP OR **KNOCK**	You need a jolt to wake up to the problem and that there is a problem to face. *(Note the area for chakra or bone concept).*
BUNION	Being stubborn and inflexible in your direction because you are not showing compassion or love for yourself. Change means growth.
BURN	You are only touching the surface of a problem and need to look for another way that is hidden under the singe. *(Note area for chakra or bone concept)*

CALLUSES	Thick skinned.
On hands	Putting up a defence to stop doing what is best for you or what you do not want to do.
On feet	Defence against changing direction.
CANCER	A form of self-destruction: Not changing concept or concepts in the area that is affected.
CAPILLARIES (Itchy in cold)	Recurring problem of only seeing the small **detail** and not the overall picture.
CARPAL TUNNEL SYNDROME	You have a fear of doing, so you block your communication from knowing the details and going against what is best for you. (spiritually, left hand or physically, right hand.)
CHILBLAINS	A recurring problem of not getting the **details** because you think you are inadequate or unworthy. Fingers - doing. Toes - direction.
CHONDROMA Benign cartilaginous growth.	It is a growing **resentment** because you think you cannot have what you want.
CORN	Keeping your concept so long that it hurts your direction. *(Use Bones Chart for actual concept)*
CRAMP (Painful contraction of a **muscle**)	**Guilty** thoughts of what you have done or have not done.
CUT	You need to look inside for answers to your problem.
DERMATITIS (Inflamation of the **skin**)	Stirred up emotions of being **unworthy** or **inadequate.**
DERMATOSIS (Any disease of the **skin**.)	Emotions of being either unworthy or inadequate which are not your true feelings. *(Take note of the area of the skin problem for Chakra concept)*
DISCS (INTERVERTEBRAL)	No feelings of **belonging.**

ERYSIPELAS (Streptoccal infection of skin - face)	Inadequate and unworthy emotions.	
FEET	**Direction** - *(See Legs or Bones concept Chapter)*	
FEET - COLD	You are not loving the **direction** you are going.If you lack courage or scared to do your direction it is as the saying suggests - "You've got cold feet."	
FEET - PERSPIRING - WET	Not wanting to be told your **direction**, you are bogged down in too much detail so you are not seeing the big picture of your direction. This is disharmony.	
FEET - PIGEON TOED	Inhibited in your **direction**. Following the direction of what you have been taught, rather than your feelings. (Your soul's plan).	
FEET - POINTED OUTWARDS (Charlie Chaplin)	**Left foot** **Right foot**	- A fear of your spiritual direction. - A fear of your physical or material direction. (When both feet are pointed straight aheadyou are balanced and sure of your direction.)
FEET - SMELLY	Your **direction** is offensive to you.	
FEET - TOES CURLED UNDER	Your direction is not balanced. You are thinkingmore of material things instead . of spiritual growth You are not controlling yourself to stop thinking you are inferior.	
FEET - WALKING ON INSIDES OF FEET	You need to plant your feet squarely on the ground and stop any thoughts of fear that you cannot face what needs to be done.	
FEET - WALKING ON SIDES OF FEET	Your **direction** is still not solid in your feelings.	
FUNGUS	Mouldy - Not changing old concepts. Need a new approach.	

GANGLION (Nerves)	**Left hand** - Not communicating and using your inflow because you have a fear of doing spiritual work.
	Right hand - Not communicating and using your inflow because of your fear of success. This is stopping your growth.
	Left foot - You are telling yourself that you are not good at something so you cannot go in that direction.
	Right foot - Not communicating to yourself that this (whatever) is the best direction for you at this time.
(Lymph)	Your **disharmony** stops your doing (hand) direction (foot).
GLANDS	**Living in the past** will affect any glands.
GRAZE	You have a problem but it will only singe you if you let it. *(Note the area for Chakra or Bone concept)*
HANDS - COLD	Not loving what you are doing.
HANDS - PERSPIRING - WET	You are thinking of too much detail and not seeing the big picture of what you are doing. You are not wanting to be told what to do. This is all disharmony.
HERNIA (Rupture)	Anger and aggression is the pressure that lets out your power from it's normal flow.
IMPETIGO (Bacteria causing red spots and crusty scabs)	Not letting go of your concepts of being inadequate or unworthy. - Arms, in your doing. Face, in your acceptance. Legs, in your direction.
INFLAMMATION (A suffix - "itis" reaction to injury - heat, redness, swelling, pain and loss of function.)	Stirred up emotions.

INSOMNIA	Your soul is not going to the universe to be recharged with energy to continue your learning here on planet earth because . . .

- You have not worked out the reasons for having the experiences you had today. You have not "unwound" by taking your mind back from the last thing you did to the first thing in the morning and seen what you have gained for yourself in your spiritual growth and also seeing if there was something you could have done better.

- You have not worked out the reasons for having the pain.

- Worrying that you will not be good enough or able to do what you need to do tomorrow.

- Not wanting to experience recurring frightening dreams because you have not interpreted them for your benefit.

- You do not want to learn.

ITCH	You have a **recurring** problem. Usually from thinking you are inadequate or unworthy. *(Note area for Chakra or Bone concept.)*
JAM	You only have a small picture of what is happening. You are not **using your full potential**. You have not understood. You have not opened up your thinking to a big picture.
JAR	You are going backwards instead of forwards.
JET LAG	You are still thinking of the past. You have not regrouped or summed up all that you learned from where you have been and cut that energy. You are not living in the present and putting all your energy into what you are doing right now.
KNOCK KNEES	You are not doing things the way you need to because you are not being yourself.
LEGS	Your **direction** ("The gait of a man is the fate of a man")
- LEFT	Your spiritual direction.
- RIGHT	Your physical or material direction.

LIGAMENTS	**Control**. You are controlling others or letting others control you or not being in control of yourself.
LUMPS	Not trusting yourself because you think you are inadequate or unworthy.
MEASLES	
Virus -	If no **peace** of mind, the **immune** system lets down it's defences.
Fever -	Children are always being **told what to do** and they are not allowed to be themselves, so they think they are **unworthy** (spots on skin) and **dissatisfied** (nose running) and cannot **say what they feel** (eyes watering).
MOLE (Naevus)	The emotion of thinking you are inadequate or unworthy from a past lifetime causes this congenital growth. *Take note of where it is situated for it's chakra concept.*
MUSCLES	**Guilt.**

- Thoughts of **guilt** about not performing to your standard.
- Worrying about other people's standards.
- Being unable to own up to something you have done or not done.

MUSCULAR ATROPHY	**Guilt** from a past lifetime.
NAILS	**Protection.**
NAILS - BITING	Wearing away your **protection**. No inner authority
NAILS - BRITTLE & BREAKING	You are not using your power for your own protection to be free and flexible to do for yourself
NAILS - INGROWING	Frightened to protect yourself by discerning your direction.
NAILS - PULLED CUTICLE	**Not following through** with what needs to be . done

NAILS - **RIDGES**	Not wanting to take that first step out of your comfortable rut or groove.
NAILS - **SPLIT**	In two minds - Uncertain or indecisive of doing (if fingers) direction (if toes).
NERVES	You are not **communicating** enough or you are communicating too much. You are over reacting.
NUMBNESS (In extremities)	No blood getting to your extremities because you are not getting the **details** of what you need to do because you do not want to do it. (Not loving what you need to **do** if arms - or your **direction,** if legs)
OBESITY	**Bottling up** emotions of loneliness, yearning etc.

GENERALIZED FATNESS:

Holding in - Wisdom, love, fears, etc.

OEDEMA	A blockage of your energy flow in whatever area you have this accumulation of serous fluid. Your negative thinking could be thinking you were not good enough or not accepting yourself in some way or thinking you cannot give out your skills.
PAIN	Not being good to yourself and giving yourself a hard time. You are going against your soul's plan.
PAPILLOMA (A benign **tumour** of the **skin**)	Not **trusting** yourself because you think you are unworthy or inadequate.
PERFUME - **OVER USE**	Not wanting to be recognized as showing what you have or how you do it.
PIMPLES	See abscess - *(Note area for Chakra or Bone Concept)*
PINS AND **NEEDLES** (**Nerves** wanting to go the best way but they are put in conflict so they twitch or tingle.	Not abiding by the rules of yourself. You are going against what you know to be right for you. And this **communication** sets you a tingling - on edge in other words. It can also be what you are not doing for yourself and the missing out puts you a tingling.

PRICK	A need to penetrate your thoughts deeper in to finding a solution to a problem. *(See Bones Chart)*
PRICK - **ROSE** **THORNS** (Poisoning)	You need to change your ways, otherwise it will "poison" you - go against you in other words.
PROUD **FLESH** (Exuberant growth of granulation tissue formed on surface of an ulcer or wound)	Not wanting to heal the concept that has caused the wound.
PSORIASIS (Whitish scales on skin)	Not casting off certain emotions or fears that go against you. Not saying your feelings.
PUS	See Abscess - *Note area for Chakra or Bone Concept.*
RASH	Irritation of your emotions of unworthiness or inadequacy. If itching, it is a problem that recurs because you have not understood why you have those thoughts.
RSI **REPETITIVE** **STRAIN** **INJURY** (**Nerves**)	You have not **communicated** to yourself what you really want or need to do for yourself. You are just doing a monotonous job which is "getting on your nerves". You are telling yourself you cannot change this situation. You have not written down your goals. Your right arm (physical or material goals) - How can I do for myself to improve my situation? Your left arm (Spiritual goals) - What can I learn from this situation? If you are not gaining or learning from what you are doing, you may as well not be doing anything - hence, no power in your arms. It is mostly to do with not doing enough to obtain your needs. (No. 3 Chakra.) Therefore competion in some way is stopping you from being one with all. Sometimes, it is not doing enough to obtain your wants (No 2 Chakra.) So, you need to be loyal to yourself.

RHEUMATISM **(Muscles)**	**Guilt.** Because of your thoughts of guilt you have stopped doing for yourself and you always put other people first.
SCRATCH	It is only a minor problem, but it will get bigger if you do not stop it now. *(See Bones Chart)*
SKIN	The emotion of inadequacy or unworthiness and not being in your true feelings. *(See Dermatosis)*
SKIN - **CANCER**	A form of destruction because of thoughts of being inadequate or unworthy.
SKIN - **DRY**	Not outflowing in your feelings. Your intellect tells you that you are unworthy to say what you really want to say.
SKIN - **PEELING**	Wanting to change your concepts of inadequate or unworthiness but not acting on them to let them go.
SPINE	You are not supporting yourself or standing up for yourself by living in your feelings. You are letting your intellect let you down.
SPRAIN Injured joint by sudden twisting or wrenching of it's **ligaments**.	You are being **controlled** by your intellect. Not having your feelings in control.
SPUR	A build up of resentment - *note where it is and see Bones Chart.*
STIFFNESS	You are rigid and inflexible in whichever area it is in. You have a resistance to change.
STINGS	Recurring problem (itch) Inadequate or unworthy. (skin)
STINGS - **BEE**	You have not told yourself that you need to look into yourself, so that you will not repeat what has been happening.
STINGS - **BLUEBOTTLES** **HAIR PLANTS** **STINGING NETTLES**	You are doing the same thing over and over and not doing anything about it.
STINGS - **SCORPION**	You need to realize you will be hurt if you do not do something about your thinking.

STINGS - WASP	You are not doing what is best for you therefore you poison yourself and it hurts.
TEMPERATURE Fever	Not wanting to be **told what to do**. Getting "steamed up" about it or it makes you boil.
TENDONS	**Inflexibility.**
TENNIS ELBOW (Muscles)	
Left Elbow	**Guilty** of not doing what is best for your soul's plan.
Right Elbow	**Guilty** of not doing for yourself. Doing for others because you think it is your duty. You have been taught to do for others before yourself.
TENOSYNOVITIS Inflammation of a **tendon**.	Need to be more **flexible**. You are not taking the plunge to do something completely different that you can enjoy.
TINEA **Fungus** between toes.	Your direction is a bit **mouldy**.
TUMOUR A swelling or morbid growth, benign or malignant.	Not **trusting** yourself or others.
ULCER	See Abscess. *Note where it is for Chakra or Bone Concept.*
VEINS	**Fear.**
VEINS - VARICOSE	You have a **fear** of some sort that is stopping you from being successful.
WAKING **BEFORE** **FULL SLEEP**	Not outflowing in the physical, therefore you do not want to regroup in the universe where you gain more insights for your growth

WAKING
NOT
REFRESHED

- You are not wanting to learn so you do not want to be awake because that is the reason you are here on earth.

- You do not want to relate to something that is worrying you.

- You do not want to be awake because you are afraid your feelings will get hurt.

- You do not want to communicate with people because they will tell you what to do.

- You do not want to face your fears.

- You are judging people and blaming them for things that you caused them to do.

WARTS

A build up of emotions of inadequacy or unworthiness. *Note area on Bones Chart.*

CHAPTER 16

THE COMMON COLD

A virus **cannot** attack you, unless you are doing these negative attitudes beforehand. Therefore, you are leaving yourself out and not being in control of yourself and acting out a few of these negative concepts. Then, the virus can get into that area.

AILMENTS	ATTITUDES THAT GO AGAINST YOU
CHEST - CONGESTED	(Chakra No.5) Submission or giving in to someone's wishes Not allowing yourself to do things **your** way.
COLD SORES	(Chakra No.1) I do not want to take in that news.
COUGHING	(Chakra No.5) You want to get rid of the emotions of not being your own master.
EARS	(Chakra No. 1) You do not want to listen to others or nobody is listening to you - intolerance.
EYES - WATERING	(Chakra No.7) Not able to say what you want to say.
HEADACHE	(Chakra No.7) Holding on to old limitations and not seeing good in anything. Thinking you are better than anyone else.
NOSE - BLOCKED	(Chakra No.1)Not enjoying yourself or what you are doing.
NOSE - RUNNING	(Chakra No.1)Not satisfied with yourself for what you have done or not done.
SNEEZING	(Chakra No.1) Not accepting yourself in a way that you feel **cheated** - you are unable to see your good points.
THROAT - LOSS OF VOICE	(Chakra No.7)You think you know more than others and it is a waste of time talking to them
THROAT - PHLEGM	(Chakra No.6) You cannot relate to someone from what they have said or done. You need a live and let live attitude.
THROAT - SORE	(Chakra No. 6)Being frustrated and not relating to yourself for not being able to have someone understand your point of view.
TEMPERATURE - FEVER	(Chakra No.1) Not wanting to be told what to do. Getting "steamed up" about it or it makes you boil!
WHEEZING	(Chakra No.5) Complaining that you cannot be yourself.

CHAPTER 17

"THE NEED TO CHANGE"

Had I not changed my thinking, I would not have this body here today. My sister's friend told her that I was the most unrelaxed person she had met. That summed me up pretty well! So I was making life very hard for myself.

My father wanted the best for me and he was a perfectionist. Whatever parents have in them, the child takes it on board some how. So the expectations I felt that I took on by his perfectionism, made me feel a failure if I did not achieve.

This is one area that needed to be changed, so I could become more relaxed and simply **be me**.

Remember those standards mentioned in Chapter 1. You can do without other peoples' standards. Have a go at these for a change: -
•   Do the best you can.
•   You are no better or no lesser than anyone.
•   Grow from everything you do.
Whatever you see in your mother or father, you could take a look at yourself and see how you do it and whether you want to change it.

Constant change is the only stable condition of life!! To be happy, a soul needs to be involved and be creative so it can keep learning and growing and changing.

We will never know it all. People complain about there being a "generation gap" - the younger generation will not communicate with their elders and vice versa. When people communicate, they need to listen, think, then speak. Listening to the other person is the way you learn, but if you think you know it all, you will not listen to the other person. Then why would the other person bother to listen to you?

YOU ARE NEVER TOO OLD TO CHANGE

If you are not wanting to be told, you will stop yourself from changing. That is not being sincere with yourself. When someone tells you something about yourself that you do not want to hear, you only need to ask your inner you, if what was said to you is the truth and if so, what percent do you do it? It may only be a couple of percent but that person has done you a favour and you need not be offended because by taking a look at yourself you can change that habit.

When you want to point out something to someone, it is best to just be an example. That is being a way shower, not a teacher.

"Don't Fail For The Want Of Trying. Give It A Go."

When first embracing spiritual teaching, this lifetime, I had to begin to put myself first and learn to do for myself and to stop catering to others as I had been taught.

How does it feel when you are doing for others all the time?
- It drains your energy and wears you out.
- You have no time to do what you really need to do for yourself.
- You may feel you are being taken advantage of.
- You could be taken for granted.
- The ones you do for can miss out on either the learning experience or the satisfaction of doing for themselves and you make them weak.

To start putting yourself first and doing for yourself first is the big transformation that most of us need to make. Just remember by learning to do for yourself first, you are helping others. They will see the change in you and want the same freedom that you are experiencing.

The reason that many people do not want to change is because of the fear of being judged. What will people think of me if I change and begin to put myself first and start loving myself and have faith in myself??? Who cares what people think! It is none of their business. Also it is none of your business to worry about what others are thinking.

You need to be caring for yourself, then those others will begin to respect you because you will have respect for yourself and they will not be able to step on your toes or use you as a door mat anymore. If everybody was minding their own business, you would not have to think that way and they would be getting on with changing themselves instead of judging you.

Do not be dragged down by these people who will not change. Move on and make new friends who want to grow and expand.

Dying is the easy way out to change! There is nothing wrong with checking out if that is what you want, but the process of your growth is lengthened because you just have to go through the baby stage again and pick up more concepts from a new set of parents and nothing is ever the same as it was, the next time round. The pity of it would be you are slowing up the process of us all becoming one.

The side effects of some drugs can help to kill you, for the simple reason, if you are being too stubborn to change, you may as well pass over and let some other soul take your space here to learn on the planet.

Does this statement give me the incentive to keep taking drugs or to start changing?

" Some Men Dream Of Worthy Accomplishment
While Others Stay Awake And Do Them."

By the same token, it is no use transplanting a new organ into a person if that person is not going to change the concept that caused the organ to cease functioning in the first place.

If that person changed the attitude that worked against him or her in that area, the new organ would be tolerated. First of all, you need to know or understand why you need to change and what concept you need to change.

If you have the pain removed, you are simply getting rid of the symptom. You then cease to look for the cause of your problem and you miss out on finding out what you need to change. No doubt you will then have the problem recurring.

The pressure of suffering, that an illness can cause is good because it is the desperation you need to force you to change. Why wait until you are desperate? Get your act together. Be brave and say "YES" to remove yourself from your comfort zone. Get out of your rut. Be flexible. Throw out tradition, if it was not designed for you or the 21st century. If anything is stopping you from being in your own true feelings or not doing what you came to do, that is a sure need for change.

Your body tells you what you need to learn - it is your barometer. Take notice of whether any part of your body is malfunctioning. Be observant where and why you were cut on that finger or why you have a corn on that toe. These are your early warning signals. *See Bones Chart for the exact concept you need to be living.*

Do not wait for whatever you are doing to yourself to overtake you. Nip it in the bud early. Look into the slightest difference in any way in your body or whether your thinking has become negative at all. Evaluate what is going on. Regroup yourself always, in other words, sum up what you learn from everything you do and see if you could do it more easily next time. Remember, no judging, only evaluating. Stumbling blocks are only stepping stones. This keeps you positive and stops you falling in a heap if you hit some blocks. There is always a solution. Even the so called bad things that happen to you, turn out to be good things because you have learned from them. The main thing to understand here, is the **changing**, not so much the change. You can then pass that knowledge on to help someone else so that they can change.

Another way to recognise what you need to change is to listen to yourself speaking about others. It could be "that person infuriates me with his pompous ways" or "I can not stand that woman, she is so negative." Whatever you see in others, you have in yourself. If what you see really annoys you, you have the concept quite badly or to a large degree. If you simply notice a concept in someone and it does not worry you, you have got over that habit. You could not notice it if you did not have it in you.

"Never Forget That Only Dead Fish Swim With The Stream."

When I first learned this technique, vandalism was annoying me. Public phones were unusable, pages torn out of the phone books, the trees on our nature strip were vandalized by children breaking the branches to pull unripe plums down just to throw them at each other.

This vandalism was annoying me so I said to my Guidance - "I'm not a vandal am I?" "Yes you are," came the reply. "You vandalize your time. You spend too much time on the phone and waste time on trivia."

Then I asked, "What can I do about what I was seeing?" You cannot change them. Change myself and teach the children. The "offenders" are simply needing to have that experience. When I realized that I have done all sorts of negative things in past lifetimes, I can't point the finger at others who are needing to learn from their deeds this lifetime.

You may not be doing it the same way as is annoying you, but you are certainly doing it in some way.

You can quietly thank those people who aggravate you because they have drawn your attention to what you needed to change and those people will not annoy you any more. You learn more from your enemies than from the people you like. Do not forget that **you attract what you need to learn.**

We are all healers. We have come to heal ourselves by learning from the innumerable states of consciousness here. Understanding and changing is healing.

Anything that stops you from **being and being at one with the universe,** such as limiting fears, guilt, worry, yearning, raciness or no self-acceptance means you need to change. When you change and shed these attitudes, and start growing, nothing is a big deal any more. You will feel good about yourself. Your body will respond and heal itself and nobody can push you around. No doubt, with change, you will begin to live in the **now, in the present** and that removes pressure from you.

Try eating a piece of fruit and just savour it with your concentration only on the eating and enjoyment of it, instead of having the mind racing off thinking of what you have to do next, etc.

The way I find a "block", which is usually a fear, is to think of what you are having trouble doing. Then ask, "If I could do that, what would I be?" Whatever you would be, that is what you have a fear of because otherwise you would be able to do it.

For example, if you cannot **communicate**, ask yourself, "How would I feel if I could communicate?" The answer could be, "I would feel that I could **show my love.**" Therefore, you have a fear of showing your love.

"Money Is Like Muck, Not Good Except It Be Spread." Francis Bacon

That is certainly not your true feeling, so meditate on how you allowed that fear into your life and just what was the experience that started this negative thinking. Once you understand where it came from, you can release it. Realize that you have allowed that experience in the past to keep you from being in your true feelings.

We work hard at keeping these concepts, why is it that we cannot work as hard at getting rid of them?

A suggestion to find out whether your direction is good. Take a look at your feet when you are standing in the shower. Are they both facing straight ahead? Is either foot facing outwards or are they pigeon-toed? Are your toes curled under or bent one way or the other? Whatever is not straight ahead, there could be something to look into to change about the direction your life is going.

Self pity is an indication you need to change as well as do-gooding or minding other people's business or fighting other people's battles.

Any signs of procrastination, indecision or loss of enthusiasm is usually due to a fear of some kind that needs to be let go and changed.
You do not have to change, but, if you do, you could find freedom. With freedom, you will need to be responsible for yourself. Why procrastinate? Procrastination is keeping up with the past!

There are some habits that you have that you can throw off as soon as you realize that they are impeding your progress. BUT, there are others that you tend not to want to let go. There are some fears and concepts from the past that just bubble up from your subconscious and rear their ugly heads when we least expect them.

If you have ever had a car accident or a very near miss, which I had while driving my five year old daughter to school. She is thirty-five now, and whenever I come to that corner, I remember that incident. This is how your sub-conscious works. When you need to make a decision of some kind, you become "wishy-washy" and indecisive, and there is that fear coming to light from some memory from 200 B.C. that is still there and you are letting it stop you from doing what you want to do. You cannot erase from your memory bank what has happened to you in the past but you can put an end to it interfering with this lifetime.

You need to understand that you have let those things happen to you and taken on these habits that are not the real you. Whatever is not you, you must let go and move on in freedom, not to be a prisoner of yourself. If you want to keep feeling like a "no hoper" keep thinking that it is hard!!!

"Pleasure And Action Makes The Hours Seem Short" Shakespeare

A few people have said to me that it is all very well knowing what concept has caused their ailment but I did not mention in my book **HOW** to change that concept.

Here are a few ways that have worked for me -

- Change to the attitude that change is simple and fun.

- You need the **inner authority** that comes from being **desperate** enough to want to change those habits to heal yourself. Determination to carry things through to completion is what is required.

- Ask your Guidance or your Inner Self to help you change.

- Tell yourself "I do not want that concept ever in my thinking again."

- Before you start any of these techniques, switch on both hemispheres of your brain by touching your right hand on your raised left knee. Then your left hand on your raised right knee and keep doing that for a couple of minutes. Look at a multiplication sign X while doing this. The X represents your corpus callosum which switches off your right brain because it does not want you to have fear, pain or fear of pain. Tell your brain that you have a choice - either to keep the concept if you enjoy suffering or rid yourself of it and be the love being that you really are and be free of that concept. Know that you have a choice.

- Let go of the concept. Put it in a bubble, or see it burning in flames and release it to the universe. Give yourself permission to dismiss it.

- Forgive the person who was in the initial experience - Never lay blame on someone else. Resentment eats into your bones.

- Forgive yourself for letting it happen. Never feel guilty. The past is over, move on.

- Recall the last time you experienced the concept. What was the emotional reaction associated with it? Put the exact opposite feeling into a positive affirmation which may begin with "I am......" (not "I can ...." or "I will ....") Make it direct and to the point. Meditate to obtain your own affirmation just for you. I do not use other people's affirmations, because we are all unique.

"He That Will Not Apply New Remedies Must Expect New Evils:
For Time Is The Greatest Innovator." Francis Bacon

- Repeat your affirmation often and project it into your vision as accomplished. Take action. Just do it. You cannot simply wait for it to happen.

- To make it less tedious, when repeating your affirmation put stress on a different word each time you say it.

- Think of how you will put this opposite feeling into practise when the habit is about to hit you again or remind yourself mentally of the positive habit replacing the old one.

- Recognize that you already are the new habit pattern.

- If the change does not happen, it could be that you are focusing on the problem too much and unconsciously you think you cannot do it and all the positive is negated. Focus on the solution and only use the problem as a marker. Get a feeling for the changed new concept, then get a feeling for the old negative one and feel the difference.

- The easiest way to change is to just be yourself and enjoy yourself and then those fears cannot "interFEAR" with your beingness.

- Make goals and know you can change if you want to.

- Have a Reiki, Ki Force or Body Harmony treatment which replenishes the energy that the fears have drained from you. Then you have the strength to combat those fears.

- Give yourself a pat on the back for recognizing that you need to change.

- Find out the exact belief you have that is causing a bad habit or concept. When you know the belief and understand where it came from, think of how stupid that belief is and how ridiculous it is and how it has been stopping you from achieving or fulfilling what you want to do. What has it cost you to keep that belief that would give you incentive to discard it and how good it would feel to change. Turn it on it's head by bringing to your consciousness all the good things you would have or gain if you let go of that belief.

- Transmute your fears or beliefs by putting them through each of your chakras. Have it in a white light. As you take it through your body, love it, honour it, embrace it and thank it for giving you it's learning experience. Now you do not need it. Say the concept at each Chakra and the loving and thanking etc. Use the concept of each Chakra for the reason it needs to leave. Put it out through your outflow chakra to the Universe and see it burning or any way of disempowering it.

"Ambition Should Be Made Of Sterner Stuff" *"William Shakespeare"*

- Keep doing this technique until you know you have a positive feeling instead of this old fear or belief. It may take you up to 20 or more times. It will leave if you want it to

I have experimented with all these ways to release old habit patterns. As of now, the last two combined, I have found to do the trick most successfully. This technique removes the power from the belief or fear and it is easy for you to check it if it rears it's ugly head again, because it has lost it's power.

If all that fails, the reason could be that you do not want to heal yourself. Then you ask your inner self for the reason or reasons why you do not want to heal yourself. Then those fears need to be worked on before you can remove the concepts causing your ailment.

This is quite a common occurance I have found. Often, the reason is a fear of responsibility or that you just do not want your need.

You need honest communication with yourself and others. This is doing for yourself so you can enjoy your stay here and make it worthwhile to live the life you wish to live with sincerity.

You may be now thinking that you need to deal with your Karma. Understand that the word **Karma** means **Action** and for every action there is a reaction. So if you have acted badly in some way towards a person in the past, you need to change the way you think. If your action was because you were impatient, you need to learn patience now. You do not have to do anything to the person involved, the Karma as you know it, will be erased simply by you changing to become patient.

Spring is a time of change and doing new things and throwing out old things. When we do that our intellect gets dissatisfied and the nose starts to run. There is the reason for hay fever being more prevalent in spring. The same happens when you release your fears. The intellect does not want to change because it has been thinking that way for a long time, so you need to be firm with that intellect or ego of yours. It does not want to lose control over you.

Police those thoughts to keep that intellect of yours well in check to do **only** the job that it is meant to do. That is to find the facts for your feelings. The intellect was designed to understand your feelings - not to talk you out of following your feelings. It is for finding out the what, when, where and why to a situation. The intellect can cause various ailments because it does not want change. It feels threatened that it is losing it's power. We have given it so much power in the past that it does not want to relinquish it. The best thing is to simply **disregard** it when it is giving you the "What ifs".

"Scientific Minds Are Trained Not To Actually Understand Reality, But Rather To Accommodate Data."

Our power to create comes from our **Feelings** NOT the intellect. The following is what could happen when you work out how to change from an old habit to being in your true feelings:-

DIZZINESS: Your intellect does not want you to be **balanced** in your feelings and intellect. The ego wants to be boss.

RUNNING NOSE: Your intellect is not **satisfied** that you want to be in your true feelings and not be controlled by your ego.

SHIVERS: Your intellect does **not like,** and feels threatened by you wanting to change to being in your true feelings.

SORE THROAT: Your intellect can not **relate** to you wanting to change from being run by your ego.

STOMACH PAINS: Your intellect does not want to **understand** that you want to run your life by your own true feelings.

VOMITING: Your intellect wants to **throw out the feelings** that you want to run your life by the power of your feelings.

The reason why your intellect closes off or switches off your creative right brain, is that in the past, you have experienced pain or fear or the fear of pain and it does not want you to go through those emotions again. Your "Corpus Callosum" (the mass of nerve fibres connecting the two sides of the brain) switches off your cerebral hemisphere, the one side of the brain that wants to do new things and be creative, so when your subconscious remembers that you have a certain fear, you are unable to make a decision. You feel helpless and "blocked", instead of just being decisive and following your feelings of knowing you can do anything if you have all the facts.

Dignity, the dictionary says, is "worthy of honour". When you have dignity, you are being yourself and living in the present. You know who you are and what you are doing here. You command respect because you know you can change and be your own master.
Dignity shuns self-pity. Changing and taking responsibility for your life makes you worthy of honour.
Move on with purpose and direction.
If you do not like the way the world is at present, start changing yourself first, then the world will change.

"Worry Is The Tradition Of The Intellect."

CHAPTER 18

DREAMS - INSIGHTS FROM REGROUPING

The soul, the real you, is attached by a silver cord to your body and every time you go to sleep, this silver cord stretches out and you, the soul, goes home to the universe to be recharged with energy. That energy is in the form of positive thoughts that you regroup what you have done and you are recharged with understanding of what you have done and when you awaken, you have this understanding in the form of pictures and symbols.

There are two types of dreams, -- prophetic and symbolic. The **prophetic** dream is the real thing. It is a picture of what is going to happen in the future.

You check with your inner self whether it is really going to happen, then what action to take.

A midwifery nurse had a dream of a peculiar caesarian birth that she had never seen before, That day she was able to use that information that she had been shown in her dream. That information had been vital to saving the life of her patient.

Sometimes you may be warned of a coming event, so you can be ready to take steps to either do it or to change things for the better. You could be told of someone else's troubles so you can warn them. The reason being that the person is too uptight to receive or hear any messages from within. (Being relaxed and living in the present is the way to be sensitive to your inner feelings and hunches). No matter who your dream is about, it is still relevant for a learning experience for you.

The **symbolic** dream is, as it's name implies, in symbols.
Firstly, there are **universal** symbols that you need to know, such as -

> Sun - Spirit or spiritual.
> White light - Spirit or spiritual.
> Water - Spirit or spiritual.
> House - Your state of consciousness.
> Baby - A new idea or beginning.
> Death - Finalization of something such as a habit or concept.
> Car - Physical direction.
> Fire - Cleansing.
> Toilet.- Outflow.
> Book - Knowledge.
> Pearls- Wisdom.
> Naked - Free or not hiding anything.
> Train - Slow direction without deviation. (on tracks)

Everybody has the same meaning from these universal symbols.

"Imagination Is More Important Than Knowledge." - Albert Einstein

Then there are the symbols that only have meaning for you. Therefore it is a good idea to have a book with a list of your own personal symbols that occur in your dreams. You could have about a hundred different symbols. It is also a good idea to keep a notebook and pencil beside your bed to write down every detail of your dream the minute you awaken. See that you do not move until you have all the details because you could break the flow before you have it in the forefront of your memory so you can write it all down before you forget.

Take note of the overall feeling of the dream which is the most important thing for interpreting your dream, then you can go over all the symbols and what each means to you.

You could dream of a person you know and they are only a symbol of their personality, attributes or their ideosyncrasies that you know they have.

If you are wanting to find an answer to a problem, make a goal to have the solution in your dream. Ask for what you want always.

If you do not interpret your dreams and act on what they are telling you, you could have the same dream recurring over and over until you do understand it.

It is the same with a nightmare, which is simply a dream which distresses you because you are not raising your level of consciousness by looking into yourself to change your bad habits. It is only distressing because you do not understand the symbols. Symbols are a kind way to tell you what you are doing or not doing to yourself. Not many of us enjoy being told. So to be told in symbols helps you to understand more clearly and it usually sticks in your memory. Then hopefully you will remember to do something about it. I know because a few of my dreams have been to tell me how silly I have acted - and those symbols I have remembered to this day.

Dreams are important for you to interpret because they are yet another way to source your information to raise your level of conciousness.

"Experience Is The Art Of Not Making
The Same Mistake Too Many Times."

CHAPTER 19

THE CAR IS THE BAROMETER
OF YOUR DIRECTION -
SO BE YOUR OWN MECHANIC!

If you have trouble with your legs, you know your direction needs to be looked into.

If you own a car and you have troubles with it, you need to look into your direction also, because your car is an extension of your direction to follow your purpose in life.

Your vehicle's style, colour, size, age and condition all reflect how you see yourself.

Think of how you feel when you drive a new stylish car. You have upgraded your thinking to a new outlook.

Red car owners want to be doing things.
Yellow car owners want to be seen.

With a large car you are making a big impression but also you carry a heavier spiritual load. A small powerful vehicle is getting you to places quickly and easily so you are decisive and achieve objectives with ease.

An old "bomb" can indicate that you are a traditionalist or stuck in a groove and not moving forward.

Your direction needs good clear energy. If your vehicle is being serviced regularly and kept clean, the chances are that you are keeping yourself healthy and doing what is best for you.

A scruffy, knocked about and damaged car represents a person who is not respecting themselves and not doing what is best for themself.

By looking at your vehicle with more detail, you can learn lots more things about yourself of which you may not have thought. If your motor is difficult to start, running rough or misfires, using excessive fuel, blowing smoke or is noisy, it may be a good idea to look into your drive and incentive which is associated with your heart area. Are you doing for yourself and putting yourself first?

To minimize repairs and extend the life of your vehicle, or any other machine you own, you have to be in **control of your own energy always**. **Speak nicely** to them. Treat them with **respect** and **love** them as any other living thing. They are your servants.

"Learning Without Thought Is Labour Lost;
Thought Without Learning Is Perilous" *Confucious*

What you need to do is to remember to ask them to perform well for you always, when you switch them on.

Tune into them and give them the attention they need.

They are an extension of your energy, therefore if you are not well, they will not be well either.

A friend of mine was loaned a car, and it just would not go for her. The owner simply got into it and off she drove in it without any garage attention.

Do not get cross with the machine, speak nicely to it. Then you will not lose your energy.

My idea here, is to give you some more insights to help you discover some more ways to make your path more smooth while you are here with this body.

Always remember that everything happens for a purpose. If you are oblivious to what is happening around you, things could keep going "wrong" until you observe and understand the reasons why these happenings are occuring to you. The summing up of these occurances give you a reason to make some changes in your life's direction. Things could start flowing and enjoyment could take over your life.

The following are a few ailments that your car could suffer and some reasons for them occuring that you could use to see what you need to change in your direction to be on the best path for your life.

"Worry Is Usually A Lot Of Trouble Which Never Happens."

ALTERNATOR

You generate your power through letting yourself just flow and you then can just **be** without putting strain on yourself to perform.

AXLE -
BROKEN

FRONT - If front wheel drive.
REAR - If rear wheel drive.
You could have a fear of your direction due to thinking you have to do things because people tell you to.

AXLE -
BROKEN

Without the wheel drive.
You are doing too much for others.

BATTERY -
FLAT

Need to rejuvenate yourself with new plans.

BIG END

You are not just being yourself to gain the power you need for your direction.

BOOT OR
HATCH WILL
NOT STAY
OPEN

You need boundaries. Boundaries are what you know you want or need. You need to tell people what they are, otherwise they do not respect your wishes

BRAKES -
WORN

Procrastination. Stopping too much and not following through on your plans.

BUMP -
INTO FRONT
OF CAR.

You are blocking your direction to grow and go forward.

BUMP -
INTO LEFT
SIDE OF CAR

You are being told with a jolt to look into your spiritual direction and learn from everything you do.

BUMP -
INTO REAR
OF CAR

A need to go forward and change yourself.

BUMP -
INTO RIGHT
SIDE OF CAR

Your physical or material direction needs to be looked into. You could be thinking you are "greater than" when communicating.

CARBURETTOR

You could be having trouble with making decisions. Follow your feelings. Do not let fears or criticism put you off.

CLUTCH - **SLIPPING**	Mental confusion. No plans for your direction.
CYLINDER **HEAD, ALSO** **CRANK CASE**	You are not doing things your way, therefore no enthusiasm for your drive to do things. That leads to lung trouble.
DIFFERENTIAL	*(See Gears)*
DISTRIBUTOR	Do not be set in your ways. Be flexible to distribute your power.
EXHAUST	You are making a lot of noise and not directing the waste outwards. Need to get rid of old habits.
FAN BELT	You are not understanding yourself which is the power you need for your progress.
FORGETTING **WHERE CAR** **IS PARKED**	Not able to find your direction.
FRONT **WHEEL** **DRIVE** **VEHICLE**	You need to know your direction **before** you apply the power. Always plan ahead.
GEARS	You are not using your discernment, consequently you will not have your enthusiasm for your drive and power to go in your direction.
GEARS **REVERSE** **NOT** **WORKING**	Not wanting to go to the past to understand the now, to move on to the future.
GENERATOR	You cannot generate anything without being in control of yourself. Then you have no outside influences.
KEYS LEFT **INSIDE** **LOCKED** **VEHICLE**	Unable to see how you can achieve your direction.
KEYS **LOCK WORN**	Giving your authority away to others.
KEYS **LOSING**	Not knowing why you are doing things. Not knowing how to find your direction.

LIGHTS NOT FUNCTIONING

BRAKE LIGHT — If you do not have boundaries, people will not know what you are doing and they will encroach on you.

HEADLIGHTS
LEFT — Not able to see your Spiritual direction.
RIGHT — Not able to see your Physical direction.

NORMAL (only high beam working) — Seeing too much but not using what you know.

HIGH BEAM (only normal working) — Not able to look ahead into the future.

INDICATOR
LEFT — You need self-acceptance to communicate what you want to do in your Spiritual direction.
RIGHT — You need self-acceptance to communicate what you want to do in your Physical direction.

INTERIOR — Unable to find solutions in adverse conditions.

REVERSE — You need self-acceptance to let people know that you can go back and look into your past without being hurt and move on in the present with understanding.

TAIL LIGHT — Not communicating what you are doing.
LEFT — Cannot communicate what you want to do in your Spiritual direction.
RIGHT — Cannot communicate what you want to do in your Physical direction.

MIRRORS — Not wanting to look back at what you have learned from whatever situation.

OIL BURNING — Inflexible - Being stuck in your old ways.

OIL LEAK — Your direction is not progressing because you are not being creative.

PISTONS & BORES — You are not doing for yourself so you can enjoy your direction.

POINTS — If you do not have self-acceptance you do not have that spark for life.

RADIATOR BOILING DRY	Getting all steamed up, then petering out with no energy.
REAR WHEEL DRIVE VEHICLE	Old habits have stopped your success. You can activate your power before you have your direction.
RUNNING OUT OF PETROL	Fear of Success. To feel abundant, keep your petrol tank always above half full.
SHOCK ABSORBERS	Self acceptance needs to be 100% and then you can overcome any shocks or knocks.
SPARK PLUGS	You are not using your own power of discernment and understanding from within to obtain your enthusiastic drive to achieve.
STARTER MOTOR	You cannot get started on your direction if you are not taking note of your feelings to just **be**.
STEERING	You are not communicating your power to do your direction.
STOLEN VEHICLE	You are not being honest with yourself and removing your fear of doing your direction.
TYRES - FLAT LEFT FRONT	A fear has stopped you being in charge of your Spiritual direction.
RIGHT FRONT	A fear has stopped you being in charge of your Physical direction.
LEFT REAR	Not putting any enthusiasm into your Spiritual direction because you are not wanting to do it.
RIGHT REAR	Not putting any enthusiasm into your Physical direction because you are not wanting to do it.
UNIVERSAL JOINT	You are not being flexible. Flexiblity gives you the power for your direction to grow.
WINDSCREEN BROKEN	Not believing that you can do your direction.
WINDSCREEN WIPERS	Not being able to see what direction you need to go.

"GUIDING OUR CHILDREN BACK TO LOVE"

This Chapter is about what I wish I had known when I had my two girls. I did the best I knew how, which was the way I was brought up. I know better now, so here are a few pointers to do what I say, not what I did!!

Bringing up our children is the most important "job" we have given to us. It is a responsibility not to be taken lightly. As the previous pages suggest, we need to learn positive qualities and respect each person as a soul. We have all come here to learn from each other. When it is loved ones, it can be a bit up hill. To achieve harmony and peace inside us and carry it out into our family, is our ultimate aim. Meditate on how it can be done.

In teaching your children all those good qualities mentioned before, you will finally have a mature adult who respects and loves him or herself, and will do the same for you and others and our planet.

I always wondered how my two children, who had the same two parents, could be so totally different. How simple that is to see now. Understanding that every soul is unique and each lifetime we choose a different set of parents. We come to learn different things from them. So why would they not be different?

Train your children to look inside for their information. It is all inside us. We must learn to tap into our source to find our own power to just be.

When you live what is in these previous chapters; "Walk your talk" as the Red Indians say, there will be no big deals when you go through a rough experience. You simply discern what the problem is and learn from it. After that there is no need to attract that situation to you again.

•   Your children learn by your example. They see that life is no big deal, when you give them understanding. That is the way to bring up your children by being an example to them. Be yourself always and allow your children to be themselves as well. If they see that you always discern a problem without making a fuss about it or make a "Federal case" out of things, they will learn to do the same. When you are cool and calm, you learn from every situation and you know there is always a solution.

•   Always be consistent and children will know what to expect of you. It is better to be a consistently "bad" parent than to be inconsistent. One way one day and another the next. That will send the child into total confusion.

"Don't Be Dim Bulbs. Be Bright Lights."   *Saint Germain*

•   Consistency between both parents does help also. The child knows who to "get round" when one parent gives in and the other wants to use discipline. These parents need to consult someone else. A person who is skilled at knowing what is good for children so they both understand the child's needs. Then they can both see that their disagreement would have a detrimental effect on the child if it continued.

•   Understand that children are old souls in new bodies. Therefore they **do understand** you. They always need explanations of your actions towards them. For instance, if you say, "Get out of here" without telling them why, the experience will create the fear of rejection in them. They will then be doing things for everybody else, just to be accepted all their life.

•   From the time your child is born, you need to show that baby that you are in charge. When you enforce your guidelines consistantly with room to grow, you will not need harsh discipline later in life. It is your house and your rules that are to be abided by while the child is here to learn from you.

•   Encourage them to keep talking to their angels, (their "unseen" playmates) unseen by you maybe but very real to children. Their Master Souls, Spiritual helpers or Guardian Angels talk to them, help them and guide them and let mothers know when the child is about to get into danger. (Mother's intuition)

This talking to imaginary friends is frowned upon by adults who tell them to stop it because they will be put in an institution if it continues. Their inner communication with Spirit is then cut off for life. That is their main source of information to know their purpose for being here and to know who they are.

One friend of mine's little grandson was telling her the names of all her guardian angels.

Another friend of mine was visiting a mother and daughter and the little girl kept pestering her mother for an icecream and whining and interrupting their conversation and would not take no for an answer. After a while, my friend just said to her, "Ask your Angels whether you need an ice cream." She just went away without another word.

There would not be all this lack of understanding between parents and children if everyone consulted their guidance for their best way to communicate.

Teach them to always look inside for their answers, then they will always be confident and follow their own feelings.

"A Good Listener Is The Wisest Of Persons."

• When you speak to children, speak to them as a soul. Do not speak down to them. Remember how it feels to be little and how big a person looks to them. If you respect them, they will respect you.

• Make sure, when giving a suggestion to your children, that they do not assume that it is a command. You are usually wanting the best for them but they could take it the wrong way, just by the tone of your voice. Tell them it is only a suggestion and not a command, if that is what it is, then you will not meet with hostility.

• If you tell your children "Don't take money from strangers" and "Money is dirty" you will give them a money hang up and they will be poor from then on.

• If you are wanting them to do something for you, tell them what it is and never tell them how to do it, (unless they ask) and then only a suggestion. Let them use their own creativity and they will feel good about doing it. If you tell them to do it your way, they will not want to do it for you.

• When they finish a job or opportunity, thank them and give them praise for what they have done. Some parents just smack them when they do something wrong and never any praise when they do it right. Children need encouragement.

• Children will not always do what you like, because they need to experience things for themselves. When that happens express your love for them but say that you do not like their actions. **Never** say that you do not love them. It is only what they have done that you do not love.

• If you see something that you do not like your children doing, stand back and see what **you** are doing or have done that may have caused them to do what they are doing. Think before you blame.

• You most probably are bringing up your children, in the same manner as your parents did and their parents did, because that is what you have learned but once you have become "Soul Conscious", you will want to change your attitude towards disciplining your children. Being seen and not heard does not help children to learn to communicate.

Help them develop their potential. They hide themselves with shyness because they are being told what to do all the time, instead of being in their feelings. Then they stop believing in what they do and say. It is easier to knock confidence out of a child than to put it back in.

"Look At My Environment And I See My Energy."

- Parents do not have to teach children their habits. Children just sense it and just naturally do the same because they are in their feelings and very sensitive. If a parent is insecure, the child will just be it also. **Insecurity** can lead to **dependency, indecision, escapism, impatience, controlling, possessive** or **knowallness**.

- As adults, our perception of love comes from our own childhood and how we experienced it when we were just feelings in our first seven years. If your father was away most of the time earning money, you think that is normal when you get married. You push a man away who is giving you too much loving attention because that is not love as you know it.
  Make sure your children are given as much love as you can possibly give them. They will thrive on it.

- Do not only hug little girls. Little boys need a cuddle also. Let them play with dolls and let girls play footie with the boys. Encourage masculine traits in girls, so they will learn to stand up for themselves and not be kept in old servile roles. They need to be balanced in either gender. The same with boys, encourage their feeling nature so they give up that domineering "he man" type role of the past and become caring. We all need to have both our feminine and our masculine traits for our future, to end this separation existence.

- Having this separation has been an **injustice**. If children let further thoughts of injustice into them, it could lead to **bitterness**, then they have no thoughts of **beingness**. Those emotions stop them from learning which affects their solar plexus. They also stop their outflow through thoughts of **inferiority** and **hostility** and then they cease to **act**. Be fair when dealing with your kids. Who wants to harbour injustice? It serves no purpose.

- You are being inconsiderate to your children if you are doing too much for them and not teaching them to do for themselves. You are taking away their opportunity to learn and grow and it makes them weak. They will become dependent on you and they will dislike you for it.

- If your children say they cannot do something, encourage them to try again. Have another go. Keep at it. Never give in. Use their creativity to expand themselves to go further. Be willing to be consistant and true to themselves and be competent. They would not have learned to walk if they had given up after their first fall.

- Give children responsibility so they can feel successful. Having responsibility also gives them a feeling of being worthwhile. Responsibility can mean to be in charge and they need to be learning to be in charge of their own lives. This stops them having thoughts that they are unworthy. Make sure they are not living by yours or other people's responsibility, only by their own.

"A Quitter Never Wins: A Winner Never Quits"

- Discipline your children with boundaries so they know how far they can go. Let these boundaries out gradually as they grow. With boundaries children feel secure. They stop them from being confused. Be consistent with your boundaries and keep them enforced until they are old enough to make their own. They will do this if they have lived by yours and have gained respect for themselves and others.

- Being overly "mothered" is as bad for the child as being neglected.

- Never be possessive parents. Everyone needs to feel free. It is love they need and lots of it - unconditional love, that is, not smother love or cupboard love. With unconditional love, they will be able to be themselves, think for themselves, make up their own minds, (decisive) and be responsible citizens.

- Give your children positive guidelines by setting them a good example. That is by **loving yourself**. This is what gives you inner strength and you want your children to have the same. So do it and they will follow.

   If children do not **love themselves**, their sensitivity picks up **criticism** and **judgment**. Then they stop **accepting** themselves and that can lead to **loneliness** or **attention seeking**.

- Judging self and others needs to cease. Each time your children get themselves in an awkward situation or go through a harrowing experience, sit down with them and work out why it has happened. Show them how to stand back from the situation and see the big picture of it all. They can then **understand** the reason for it happening. This all has a calming effect and they can then see that there is no need to blame and judge whatever and live and let live reigns supreme. That stops them carrying grudges and injustices and unforgiveness, which all stems from judging.

   This regrouping of their experiences starts them learning from all their situations and they grow from them.

- Children from 0 to 7 years never hold grudges. They can be spanked and mistreated by a parent and they will very quickly give that parent a big hug as though nothing has happened. I call this recycling their love and we can learn from them. At that age they are always in their feelings and simply being themselves. When something adverse happens to them they just get back to loving again.

   Not like adults, they hold on to grudges and want revenge and want to keep retaliating, with never a thought for forgiveness. This all eats into your bones and bodies and that is how your sickness begins.

"Nothing Happens To You That You Cannot Handle."

• Your children mainly get sick because parents are inconsiderate to them. They do it to make the parents suffer. It is their way of rebelling. They do not realize that in doing this, they are the ones being hurt.

• Do not treat your children as toys. You have a precious soul whose character you help to mould.

• Listen to your children's feelings and learn from them how to get back into your own true feelings. See the **elf** in **S-elf**, and put some fun in your life.

• Communicate with your children. If you do not, it will lead to confusion and then conflict. Remember you are learning from your children at the same time as they are learning from you.

The sooner you find out, what you each are here to learn from each other, the better you will help them.

• Here is a no no of which some parents are guilty. When someone speaks to your children, please let the children answer for themselves. Do not jump in with your answer, as is often the case. If children are not given a chance to speak when little -- any wonder there are communication problems later on.

• When they want an answer to a question, give them the right answer. They would rather not be given nonsense or fairy tales. Do not be afraid to tell them the truth. Have respect for them. They have good memories you know and they will hold it against you. Take the time to explain things to them.

• If they have been encouraged to listen for their inspirations and follow their hunches and feelings, they will know what profession they wish to follow. Then they will be happy doing what they need to do.

• If siblings are showing hostility towards one another and nothing you do or say stops them, I suggest you mentally and visually put a white light over them and mentally send love to them as often as you can.

If they are still not showing any compassion to each other, find a Reiki II Channel for a distant healing. You would then find out the cause of no compassion and a change could be brought about. Hostility drains your energy as it takes more energy to hate than to love. It is imperative that you solve this problem by understanding the reason for the fighting because it is happening for a purpose.

"Tradition Stops Growth."

144

• Watch your words or rather listen to your speech when talking to children. Words are vibrations, say them often enough and what you say will manifest. Therefore, the more positive your words, the more power you convey.

DISEMPOWERING and EMPOWERING SPEECH

Should	Can or could
Must	I would like to.
Have to	Do it for me and enjoy it.
Can't	I will do my best.
Try	Just do it.
Too hard	I don't know how but I will learn.
I can't afford it	My priorities are somewhere else.
I can't believe it	Believe it.
Don't forget	Please remember.
Don't drop that	Hold on tight and be careful.
I'm sick and tired	I've had enough or need a change.
I'm dying to	I really want to or I would like to.
Silly me	I could do better.
Bad shot	You've got work there!I could improve.
I'm too busy	I will make time.
Blow my mind	That is amazing.
I can't wait 'til....	I will be so happy when....
I don't deserve this	I am worthy of the best
You are a pain in the neck	Your actions could be better.
I don't think I am this lucky.	I deserve the best.

If you are often being sarcastic, people may not know when they can believe you.

• When you first say "NO" to a child, that is the beginning of limiting their creative abilities. That is the start of a big disempowerment. Explain your reason for saying "NO."

• From 0 to 7 years, children are simply in their feelings and their personality is being formed in this cycle. Then they are sent to school and in the 7 to 14 years cycle, they start using their intellect. Usually, their schooling squashes out their feelings and the intellect is trained to take over.

Parents can help here by always asking their children how they **feel** about things. Not what they think about things and how they are being taught to think.

Bring their inner feelings to the fore. Encourage them to keep listening to their inner Guidance for their inspiration and help.

So many people are doing what their parents want them to do. Is it any wonder we have so many disinterested, unhappy people.

"What We Have To Learn To Do, We Learn By Doing."

145

• You create more aggression if you permit children to play at attacking each other with weapons. Make your children proud that they do not need them. Do not be forced to give in by peer groups. Organize other parents and form groups to stand up against weaponry. Do not limit yourself in what you can attain. Ask for help.

Business thrives on wars and it is business that controls the world. It is business that is against the utilization of the sun, wind and waves and use of these free non polluting sources of energy.

Healthy competition of games like the Olympics began so that men would steer their aggressive warring energy away from war.

• Everyone in a household needs to share the responsibilities so that it is running smoothly. Have round table conferences with the list of opportunities of what is required and let each member of the family choose what they like doing and to their ability and their fair share. Show appreciation for a job well done. You cannot force children to like doing something unless they are doing it for themselves. They need to get something out of it for themselves. Their incentive and enthusiasm must come from inside them.

Pay them at the end of the week if they have completed their opportunities. Money is an energy exchange. Do not just give it as an "allowance." They will learn to respect it as it has been earned.

• When your children have flown the nest, are you still possessive of them? When they come to visit you, do you treat them as you would a normal visitor or do you tell them off as though you are still bringing them up?

You do not own children. You have had many many different parents in your past lifetimes so how could you. Everyone is their own person, a unique being and is one with every being on the planet.

• You as parents are given this chance to see that your children are allowed to blossom into their own uninhibited creativity with self confidence to do what you have not yet done in these fast changing times. Do not hold them back with traditional learning. Let them express themselves and be open to let out their wisdom for they are remembering how the world used to be and they will bring the changes to be implemented.

• Discipline keeps children feeling secure.

"Experience Is Not What Happens To A Man; It Is What A Man Does With What Happens To Him"   - Aldous Huxley.

INDEX

147

148

149

INDEX FOR CAR AILMENTS

Addendum

ADRENALIN
(Chakra 2)

Was originally a survival mechanism which is rarely used now. If adrenalin is produced through anger or fear and is not used, our thinking becomes **confused**. **Action** is required to do something with that energy such as walking, running or exercising.

AMENORRHOEA
NO PERIODS
(Chakra 3)

Love - Teaching - Spiritual.
1) A symptom of anorexia.
2) Use of Contraceptive pill.
3) No love of self in a way that I do not think that I can see myself wanting to be true to myself. I need to listen to my inner more so that I can know my inner essence.

ANEURYSM
(Chakra 5)

Not loving yourself because you feel cheated and you do not want to move on.

APNOEA
(Chakra 1)

(A temporary inability to breathe.) I will not be able to face whatever I am doing. A lack of self acceptance.

AURICULAR
FIBRILLATION
(Chakra 5)

Irregular cardiac action
Fear of success.

COMPULSIVE
SPENDING
(Chakra 1)

Lack of self acceptance.

EYE BROWS
TWITCHING
(Chakra 7)

You do not want to see how you are not using your inner knowings so that you will be successful.

EYES
DETACHED
RETINA
(Chakra 7)

Could be any of three concepts.
• **Impatience** with others who cannot see your point of view.
• **Self Acceptance**. You are not accepting yourself when you go out of your immediate safe environment.
• **Inflexible**. You are inflexible when stating what you want.

EYES
GLAUCOMA
(Chakra 7)

You are putting pressure on yourself by thinking you are greater than and you are bottling up this feeling. Change to seeing the good in others so that you feel at one with people. You must realise you are no better than anyone else.

GIGGLING

It starts when you do not know what to do in a situation.

LEAKING
VALVES

You need to be **assertive** with either your spiritual growth or physical life.

MENINGITIS
(Chakra 1)

Needs freedom without restrictions. *addition to p57.*

Addendum

NAILS - WHITE
BLOTCHES
A good **perception** of yourself is needed and to accept yourself for your **protection**.

PERIODONTITIS
Bacteria of the gums inflammation.
Needs creativity for progress to get things done.

POST NATAL
DEPRESSION
(Chakra 3)
Love - Teaching - Physical.
Not one with all.

RESTLESS LEGS
(Chakra 1)
Nerves - Communicate your need to discern your direction.

STROKE
(Chakra 1)
another reason - Resisting spiritual growth.

SUN SPOTS
The sun has changed and the radiation from the sun is different. Sun cancers are a result of your inability to adapt to the changing conditions. The new sun is for the new age thinking, different from the old age. Those people who embrace the new thinking will have little or no problem with their skin. Those who resist that change will have change thrust upon them.

TATTOOS
(Chakra 7)
You want to be recognized (glory). When you believe in yourself you do not need to blemish your body.

TICKS
You need to use your discernment.

WHOOPING
COUGH
Being controlled by someone so you want to get rid of the emotion of not being your own master.

Electric fans spin clockwise, therefore it goes against our chakras which spin anticlockwise. It is best not to be directly under one for your aura's sake

Your system needs body temperature. If you have **hot showers**, your body gets over heated and your **endocrine systems** go into a state of closure.

A suggestion to help you enjoy whatever you do. Before taking action, ask yourself "Am I doing this action from **love, toil or manipulation**?" If it is from the latter two, decide what is the reason and change it.

CAR FUSES
BLOWING
You are putting too much energy into one situation without discerning the big picture.

CAR SPEEDO
Look into your timing.